Written by Mark Colenburg
Edited by Joe Bergamini
Book design and layout by Rick Gratton
Cover Design by Mike Hoff
Music transcriptions and engraving by Rick Gratton
MIDI/Finale audio examples created by Willie Rose
Photography: Cheryl Herman
Executive Producer: Rob Wallis

Video Credits:

Directed and Edited by Alfonse Giordano
Filmed and Recorded at TKL Studios
Recording/Mixing/Mastering Engineer: Blair Wells
Assistant Engineer: Dane Colón
Cameras/Lighting: Greg Tysh
Video Recording: John Cariddi
Drum Techs: Daryl Anderson and Greg Crane

Music:

Produced by: Mark Colenburg, Chris Sholar
Mixed and Mastered by: Blair Wells
Special Guest Artist: Chris Sholar (Vocals, Guitar, Keys)
Programming, Drums, Aux Keys: Mark Colenburg
Additional Musicians:
Keyboards: Cory Fuller (track 4)
Written by: Mark Colenburg^, Chris Sholar*
Mac Burg Music (ASCAP), Emoni-Miles Music (ASCAP)

1. Code^*
2. Resolved*
3. Swaggestry^*
4. Unlocked^

THE BEAT MATRIX UNLOCKED

Loops/Samples (audio only):

Produced by: Mark Colenburg and Blair Wells

Special Thanks to Tom Lewandowski and Mike Maresca, Yamaha, Zildjian, Vater Percussion, Remo, and Arturia for their quality instruments and support.

For more information about Mark Colenburg, please visit **www.markcolenburg.com**

For information about the Hudson Music catalog of educational products for musicians, please visit **www.hudsonmusic.com**.

HUDSON MUSIC®

THE BEAT MATRIX UNLOCKED

Preface 4
Introduction 5

BEAT CONCEPTS 7
The Beats 7

WARM UP 10
Warm Up #1 10
Warm Up #2 12
Warm Up #3 13
Warm Up #4 14
Warm Up #5 15

PATTERNS 16
The 10 Essential Beats 17
Study #1 19
Study #2 20
Study #3 22
Study #4 23
Study #5 24
Drum Melodics 25
Expression 26
Study #6 27
Study #7 28
Study #8 30

SONICS 32
Study #9 33
Study #10 34
Study #11 35
Study #12 37
Study #13 (The Loops and Sample Section) 38

MUSICAL SWAG 39
Study #14 40
Study #15 41
Study #16 43
Study #17 44

PERFORMANCE 45
Study #18 46
How To Move Music: Hi-Hat Patterns, Anticipations, Accents 47
Crazy Combinations with Accents and Triplets 52
Hand to Hand 53
Study #19 54
Study #20 The Power of the Loop 55
Study #21 Live vs. Studio 56

IMPROVISATION 57
Study #22 Improv Exercises 58
Study #23 Discover Your Voice 60
Study #24 Defining Your Voice 61
Study #25 Inspiration 62
Study #26 63
Study #27 Comping 65

CHOP CLASS **67**
Study #28 Chop Language 68
Study #29 Independence 71
Study #30 Tension and Release 75
Study #31 Repetition, Call and Response 77
Study #32 Inversions 82
Study #33 Punctuations 84
Study #34 Vocabulary 87

SOLOING **88**
Study #35 89
Study #36 92

AMALGAMATION **93**
Study #37 93
Study #38/#39 96

PLAY-ALONG **100**

THE MATRIX UNLOCKED BPM **103**

ABOUT THE AUDIO/VIDEO

To access the included audio and video files, go to **www.halleonard.com/mylibrary** and enter the code found on the card insde the back of this book.

Each example has a matching audio file. They are numbered to match the book. For the digital book, click on the example number to hear the file.

Play-Along Tracks (w/video)

• Each with and without drums.
• One-bar click count in for tracks with no drums.

1. Code
2. Resolved
3. Swaggestry
4. Unlocked

DRUM KEY

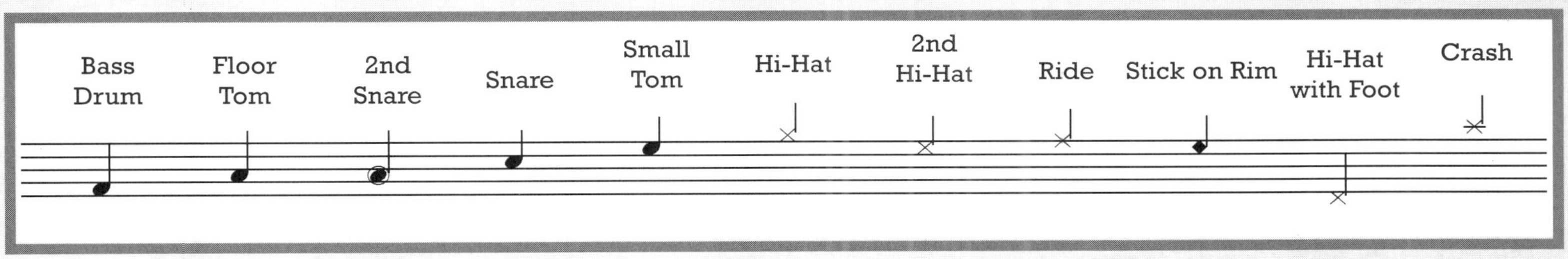

PREFACE

Welcome to our world!

Thank you for your inspiration to keep growing as a musician. It is the reason behind this presentation, and I'm honored to share my experiences and go on this journey with you.

Here is what happened to me:

I used to wonder why when I played beats live it didn't feel or sound like the record, there was a lack freedom to be creative, I was frustrated to take a solo, feeling very limited and that what I'd play really didn't fit. Imagine you had to perform some music from a record that was made with programmed beats (or sounded like it). You really liked the music and were excited to play it. You gave your very best effort in practice and the performance only to discover how disconnected everything felt, and that no matter how hard you tried, what you played felt like it wasn't authentically fitting the music. There is a struggle, a feeling of knowing there is more and you really want to pursue it. This is how I felt for a while and is why I wanted to share some of my lessons on this continual journey with you.

The musical start for me happened by playing drums in church. From there it went to learning about jazz, leading me to hip-hop, R&B, rock, and eventually to mixing them all together. Through the years I've gained a lot of experience and discovered there's a similarity to all these types of music that links them. I had been a student of every band offered in school from elementary through high school, including gospel choir, symphonic band, concert band, jazz band, pep band and marching band. Then I moved to New York City to continue my jazz studies, which embodied and built on the things I learned in school. What I wasn't expecting was to be introduced to a person whose musical concept would change my musicianship forever: James Yancey, a.k.a. J Dilla.

In that first year in New York, I had the opportunity to play in a band and recreate some of Dilla's programmed beats live from the game-changing hip-hop album *Like Water for Chocolate* by the artist Common. It was my first major tour. Upon hearing that album my first thought was, "Wow, these drums sound so live even though they are programmed, I want to learn more." On further study, I discovered that the only drummer I had ever heard play hip-hop was on that album. It was Questlove.

Growing up, when I heard beats I'd often shrug and think, "Eh, it's just a beat, I can do that." But after going back and forth listening to Questlove and Dilla, I learned that there is a lot more happening than just playing a beat. I then discovered that there were musical treasures down this road and I wanted all of them.

There are three basic concepts of this puzzle that I would like to highlight and share with you. They are **beats**, **improvisation**, and **exploration**. It may sound simple, but this study has significantly enhanced my musicianship and caused me to recognize more depth in music than I ever thought possible. This has helped me start the quest to unlock what I call *The Beat Matrix*. Musical artists like Kendrick Lamar, Flying Lotus, Karriem Riggins, Snarky Puppy, Robert Glasper, Thundercat, Christian Scott, and many others are either fusing the idea of taking beat concepts and turning it into organic music, or taking organic music and applying it to programmed beats. This is opening endless possibilities on what music can do, how far it can go, and the experience the listener can have.

We will explore how beats can be used more as a musical concept that can mix with and enhance any genre, as well as the other way around. This ultimately will allow you to push the music further, compete with technology, blend different music languages authentically, and result in being a better musician of today for tomorrow.

INTRODUCTION

The Quest

The Beat Matrix Unlocked is designed to properly musically educate, and broaden your perspective in the art of "beats" (programmed or sampled music) and musicality, as it pertains to the drum set. The big wave that's happening now with how beats are used in music is ever changing and expanding, calling for higher education and demands. Due to this surge, I strongly felt it was important to share my knowledge and experience in this area, to meet this need. In this project I will focus on some of the concepts that I've learned from a few different producers (mainly J Dilla), along with my other musical experiences playing drums in various genres over the years.

The goal is to show a more organic approach to understanding the possibility of beats and their application on the drums. These concepts can be used in different genres, songs, solos, or just playing grooves. When learned and applied, they can take musicality to another dimension and significantly enhance the player, whether solo or with a band. Be sure to catch the **"keys"** as they help you unlock this matrix!

Outline

As we proceed through the book, we'll follow this basic outline:

1. **Beat Concepts** - The beat, patterns, sonics, feel and performance
2. **Improvisation** - The voice, chops, and soloing
3. **Amalgamation**- The swag, the blend, and freedom

Each chapter of the book will expand on these three basic sections.

Setup

Here is the kit that I'm using for this session. Every piece here is to expound upon some of the concepts that I use when I play music.

- 20" kick
- 14" snare (2nd snare optional)
- 12" Tom (10" tom optional)
- 16" Floor Tom
- Hi Hat
- Ride
- Crash
- Cymbal Stack
- Electronic Drum Pad (optional)

You don't have to have this set up. If you don't have an electronic pad, or stack, or anything like that, you still can practice these concepts and learn the principles that I'm showing you.

INTRODUCTION

The Flow

These studies will unfold in three basic operations.

1. **Concept:** This will be geared towards explaining the concept and showing how it works. Spend as much time as needed to understand the concept as it is what will add to your musical growth.

2. **Exercises:** These are meant to be repeated over and over to ingrain the concept.

3. **Creative Practice Time (C.P. T.):** Everything connects to practice in some way, but creative practice in particular is time that you intentionally take to incorporate the concepts learned. Feel totally free and have fun throughout every study and exercise.

> "What you do in practice is what you will do in the performance."
> Try to become the person you would like to be on stage in the practice room.

Good Practice Tips

• **Record yourself**. It's great to have something to record yourself but if you don't, know that your brain is the best recording system you have. Having said that, recording yourself helps you hear what you're really doing, because when you are practicing and thinking at the same time, there can be some deception in what you're playing and what's actually being played. So, recording yourself helps you hear the actual notes being played.

• **Repetition is key.** I've been asked how much a person should practice.

Setting time aside and dedicating it to working on things is great, but don't allow it to stop there. In your mind you can practice at any time, as well as tapping your hands and feet. Take full advantage of all the time you have. Music is 24/7. And the more you are in the state of thinking about music, the more you're able to stay in the flow of practicing. When you do set time aside, that's where you focus on whatever concepts that you want to apply. It could be three hours, eight hours—any amount of time. It's a good way to cut out all of the clutter in life and focus on music.

> "Practice never stops."

• **Growth takes time.** The finished product doesn't happen overnight, but growth does. Always know that as long as you're sticking with it, you are growing.

• **Mistakes can be productive**. Something that I've learned from Dilla and other producers is that every note matters, even mistakes, because where the notes fail, intention can make up the difference. So always give it 100%! It may not feel good, but, from mistakes, you're able to learn, not only about the correct way of whatever you're trying to be good at, but also showing honesty in the moment.

• **Set goals**. Set a goal to be able to do something you couldn't do before, or know something you didn't before—and again, for it to stick, repetition is the key.

So let's dive in!

BEAT CONCEPTS

The Beats

Often, beats are thought about in terms of hip-hop, but there is more to understand. I've also discovered that thinking of beats more from a musical concept opens the possibilities when applying them to the drum set. Thought, motion, sound, and patterns are the basic way of opening up the musical horizon. Anything combining these elements can be considered a beat even if it is on another instrument.

Although the concept of drum programming has been around for a long time, here are some of the producers that I first heard program drums as if there was a live drummer playing (i.e., not sounding so much like a loop) that changed my musical perspective. Also, I want to showcase an example of a live drummer playing like a programmed, produced track. This not only opened up the concepts of programming drums but also how a drummer can approach playing the acoustic drums.

Here are some notable beats with transcriptions. We will then explore some of the concepts learned from them and more in the chapters to follow.

> "Programmers emulate real drummers concepts and ideas" so we're already ahead!

Diana In The Autumn

♩ = 98 BPM

Artist: Gap Mangione

Drummer: Steve Gadd

1\. This groove was sampled and used in the J Dilla track "Fall in Love."

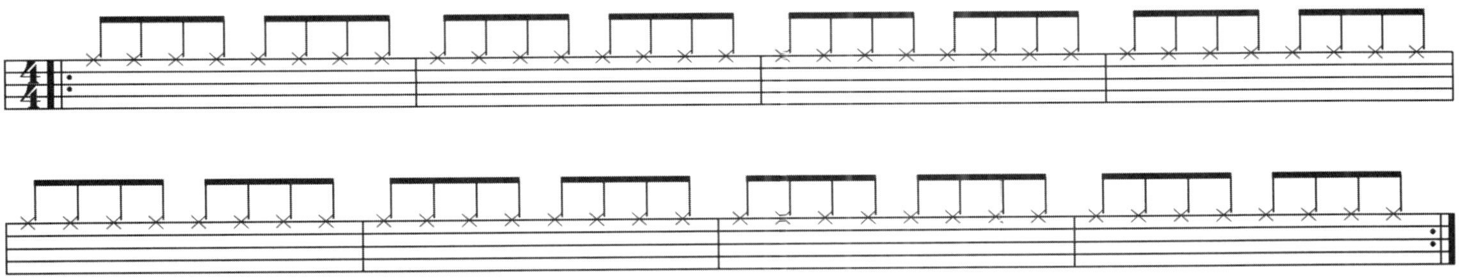

Fall In Love

♩ = 93 BPM

Artist: J Dilla

Producer: J Dilla

2\. Note the creativity in the use of the loop.

Wonderin

♩ = 107 BPM

Drummer: Roy Haynes

Artist: Roy Haynes

3.

This groove was sampled and used in the Q Tip track "Higher"

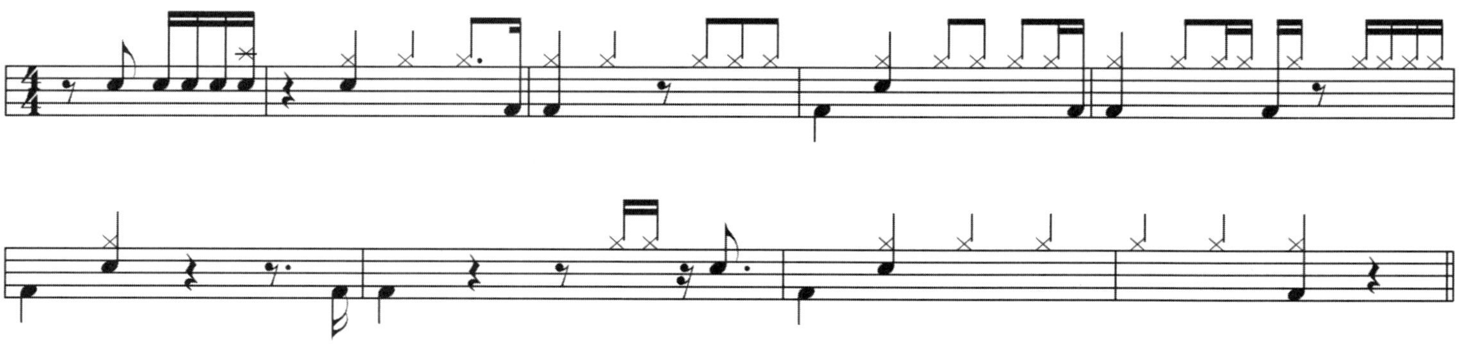

Higher

♩ = 94 BPM

Producer: J Dilla

Drum Program: J Dilla

Artist: Q. Tip

4.

This track uses a sample of the Roy Haynes drum track from "Wonderin'." Note the sonics and variation.

One in a Million

♩ = 61 BPM

Producer: Timbaland

Drum Program: Timbaland

Artist: Aaliyah

5.

Note the complexity of this beat. This embodies the concept of showing skills but having a strong beat.

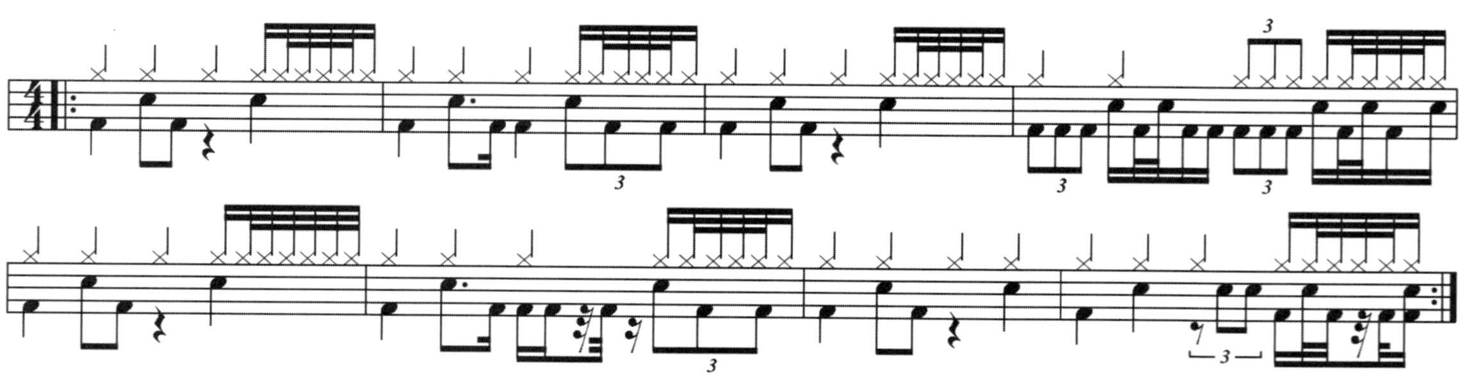

BEAT CONCEPTS

Rock With You

♩ = 114 BPM

Artist: Michael Jackson

Producer: Quincy Jones
Drummer: John Robinson
(Note the subtle kick drum variation that makes all the difference!)

6.

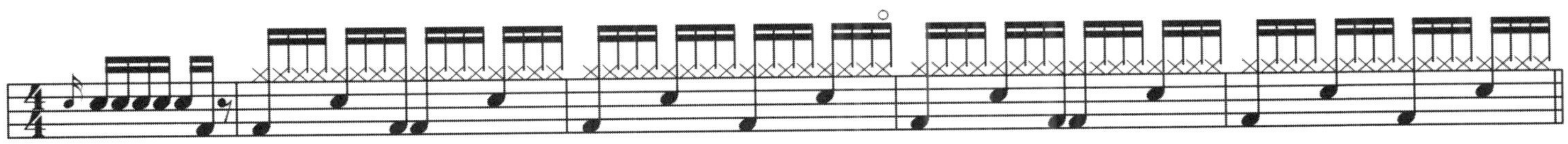

All Falls Down

♩ = 91 BPM

Artist: Kanye West

Producer: Kanye West
Drum Program: Kanye West

7.

Note the feel and hi-hat syncopation.

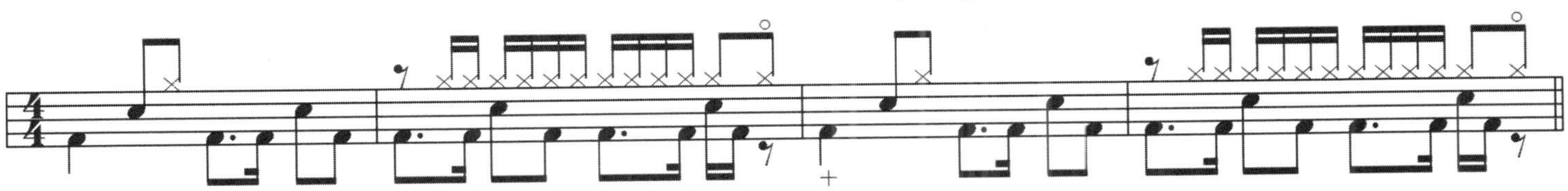

Bang Bang Bang

♩ = 92 BPM

Artist: Mark Ronson

Producer: Mark Ronson
Drums: Homer Steinweiss

8.

Note the linear approach.

Shape Of You

♩ = 96 BPM

Artist: Steve Mac

Drum Program: Steve Mac, Ed Sheeran

9.

Note the simplicity.

Trap Beat

♩ = 70 BPM

Artist: Various

Producer: Various

10.

These can be very complex

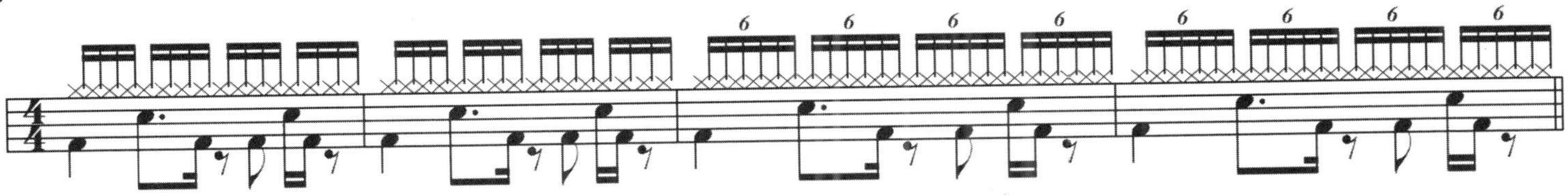

WARM UP

Warm Up #1

This will be a full journey so let's prepare for the quest. These exercises will help to get the limbs loose and the mind in sync, and have you ready to play.

I call this the **7-way exercise** because 7 things are being worked on at the same time.

1. Mind
2. Independence
3. Groove
4. R.H.
5. L.H.
6. R.F.
7. L.F.

Tip - **once this becomes too easy, try to create a new one. Doing this will cause your mind to focus on the exercise again, making it sharp and ready to play.**

11.

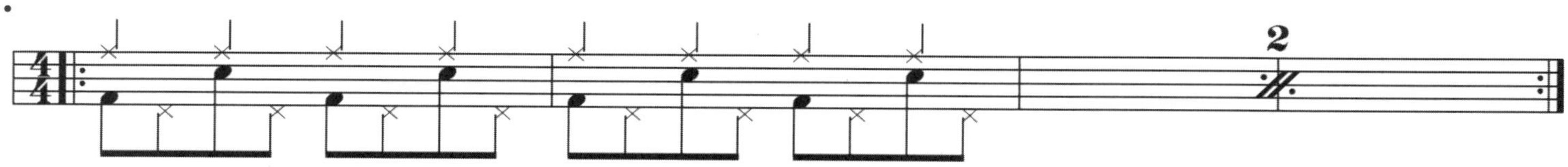

12.

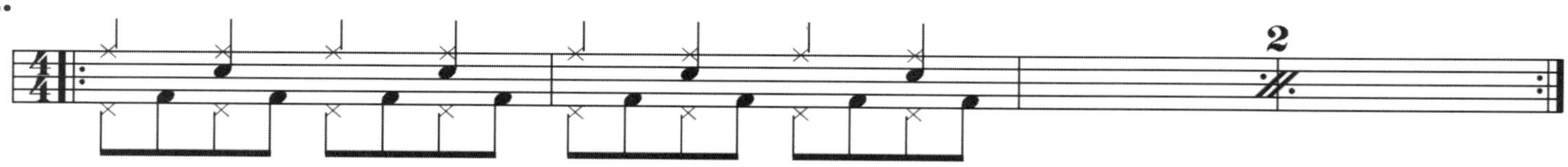

13.

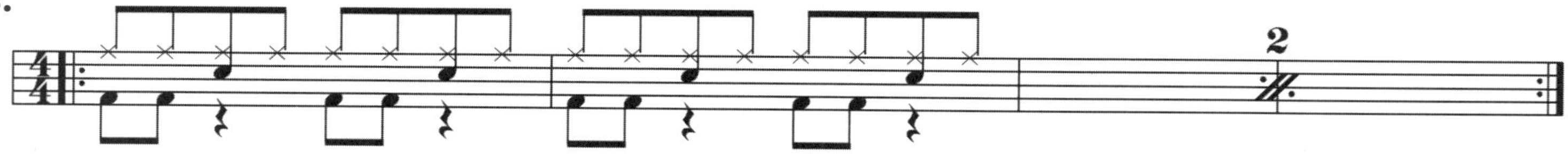

14.

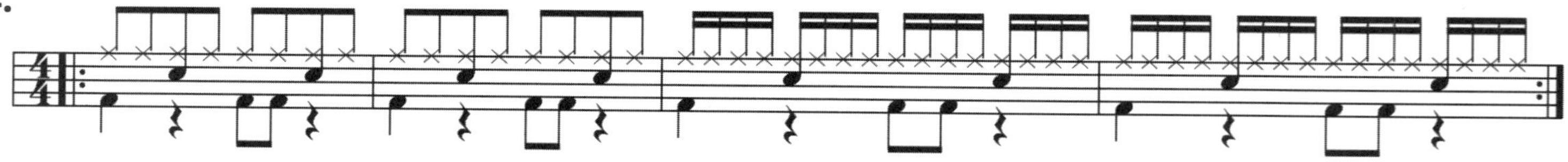

WARM UP

Now, some of this may seem simple. But the challenge is to make sure that there's a steadiness in the coordination and a consistency in sound and tempo. Pay special attention to when the hi-hat hand switches from eighths to sixteenths. Going through some of these concepts, and exercises like this, will help create a balance and facility in playing grooves.

Warm Up #2

Here is a warm-up I use for the hands, comprised of single and double strokes. This warm-up is about focusing on the hands with the groove. The focus here is to keep all the notes at the same consistency and volume level.

Tip - **practice in front of a mirror to observe your hand technique.**

15.

16.

17.

18.

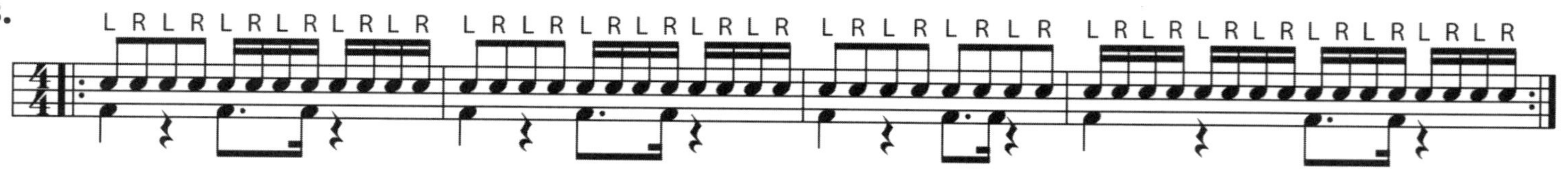

19.

WARM UP

Warm Up #3

Here the idea is to use syncopation to free up from playing straight. In these examples, we keep a constant beat between the snare and the bass drum while varying the hi-hat part. This will give freedom to the lead hand when creating beats.

20.

BASIC BEAT

HI-HAT PATTERNS

21.

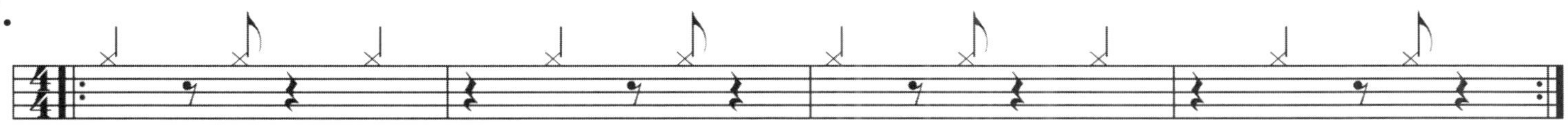

22.

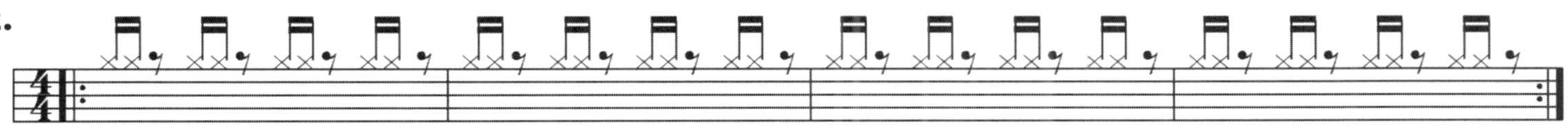

23.

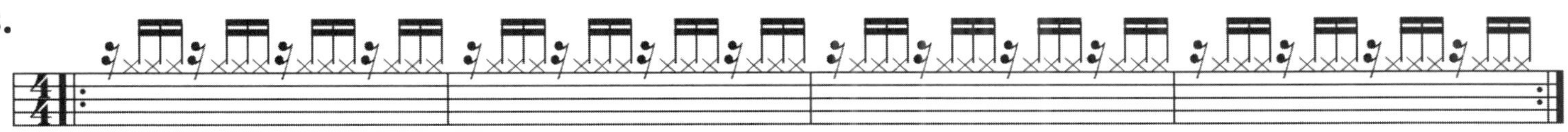

24.

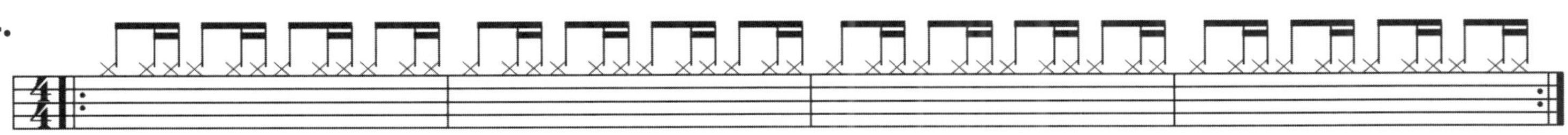

25.

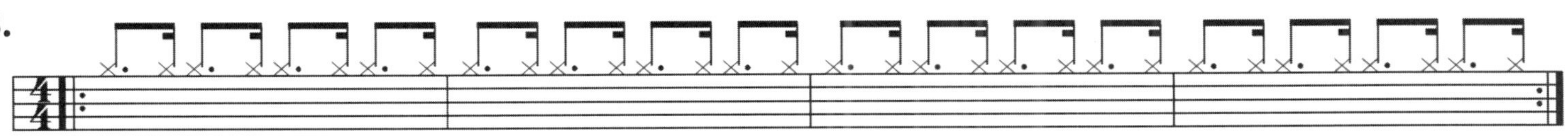

26.

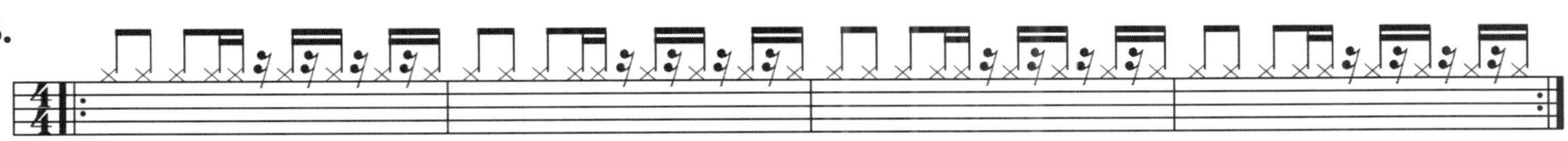

27.

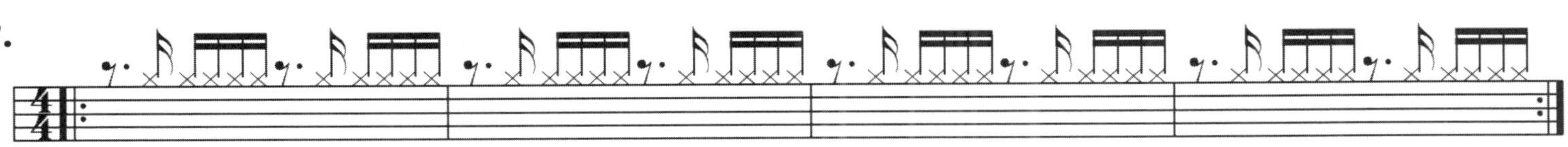

Warm Up #4

The idea here is to have any limb be able to lead. These exercises are a little tricky because the rhythmic rate of one limb changes while the basic beat stays constant. Examples 28 and 29 should be practiced individually and then put together. Pay attention to keeping the kick and snare consistent as the hi-hat part changes.

28.

BASIC BEAT

HI-HAT PATTERNS

29.

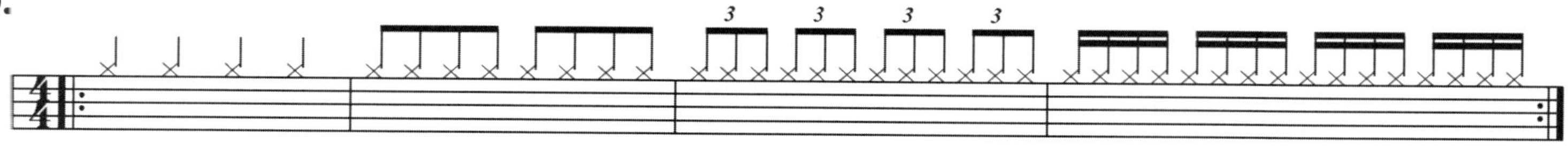

In the next example of this, we're going to keep eighth notes on the hi-hat and keep the bass drum pattern pattern the same, but do all the rate changing with the snare hand. **The** goal is to try to keep the snare still hitting at full volume and **not** to ghost the snare.

30.

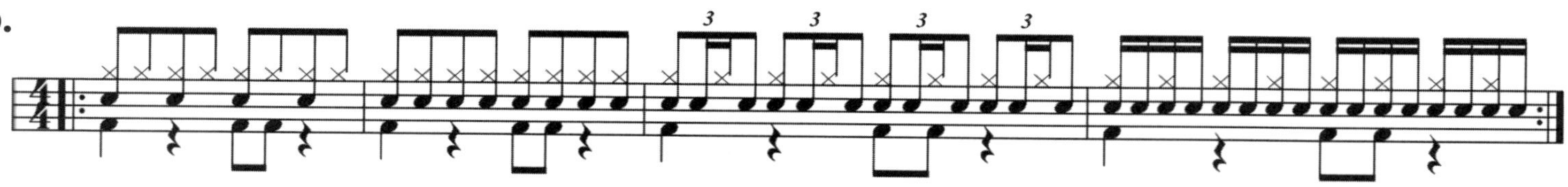

And finally we'll take the same concept but do the rate changing on the bass drum. So we're going to have eighth notes on the hi-hat, quarter notes on the snare, and we're going to change the rate on the bass drum.

31.

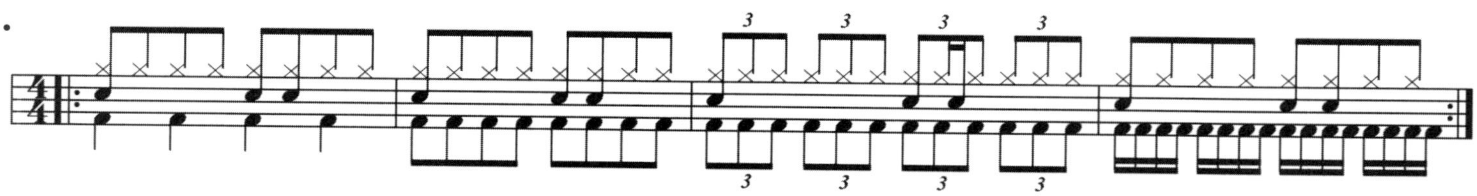

Exercises like this will develop your ability to have any limb lead.

Warm Up #5

After going through the warm-ups, the final step is to just play! Don't worry about being so technical. Keep in mind some of the things we've gone over, but then deviate from them and be creative. And just have fun. This is an important part of practice: just having fun and just playing. Because, in the moment, when you're in a situation where you're playing, whether in school, a live show, in the studio, playing a song, in that moment, it's good to know how to be free and not to think about anything—and you should practice doing that.

"Practicing freedom creates the ability to express musical freedom when playing live." This is very healthy. From fills, soloing, etc. just play, but keeping a beat going helps the mind focus and provides rhythmic context and musical purpose.

32.

FREEDOM

JUST PLAY

HAVE FUN

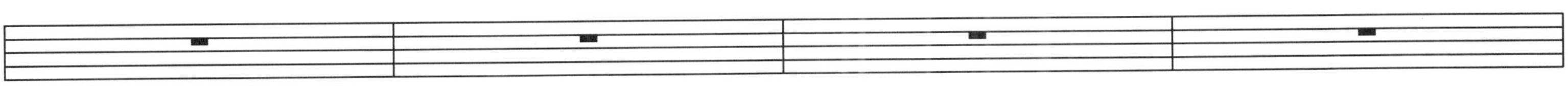

GO AS FAST OR AS SLOW AS YOU CAN

KEY - IT'S OK TO PLAY"

PATTERNS

When I think about playing drums, even in a band setting, the drums can literally play a song in themselves. The parts speak to each other and create a conversation that sings in its own unique way. It's important to be able to hear the conversation in the drums and feel the mood that is created when listening to the parts. What this does is gives life and meaning to the beats played, rather than just playing notes.

"A beat = a song." (rhythm has a melody)
"Just because our voice is different, doesn't mean we're less creative, catchy, or important".

Master Key "The Power of Simplicity"

One thing I've learn from producers, J Dilla in particular, is how powerful simplicity is. It's really about cutting out all of the clutter and focusing on the few things that really matter, that in and of itself sounds simple. Examples of simple would be time, a pattern, a sound, or even just being able to nod to a beat. If the basics are not achieved, then everything else lacks true meaning and purpose—and this is easily spotted by the listener and other musicians. That's what separates the real "pros" from the "nos."

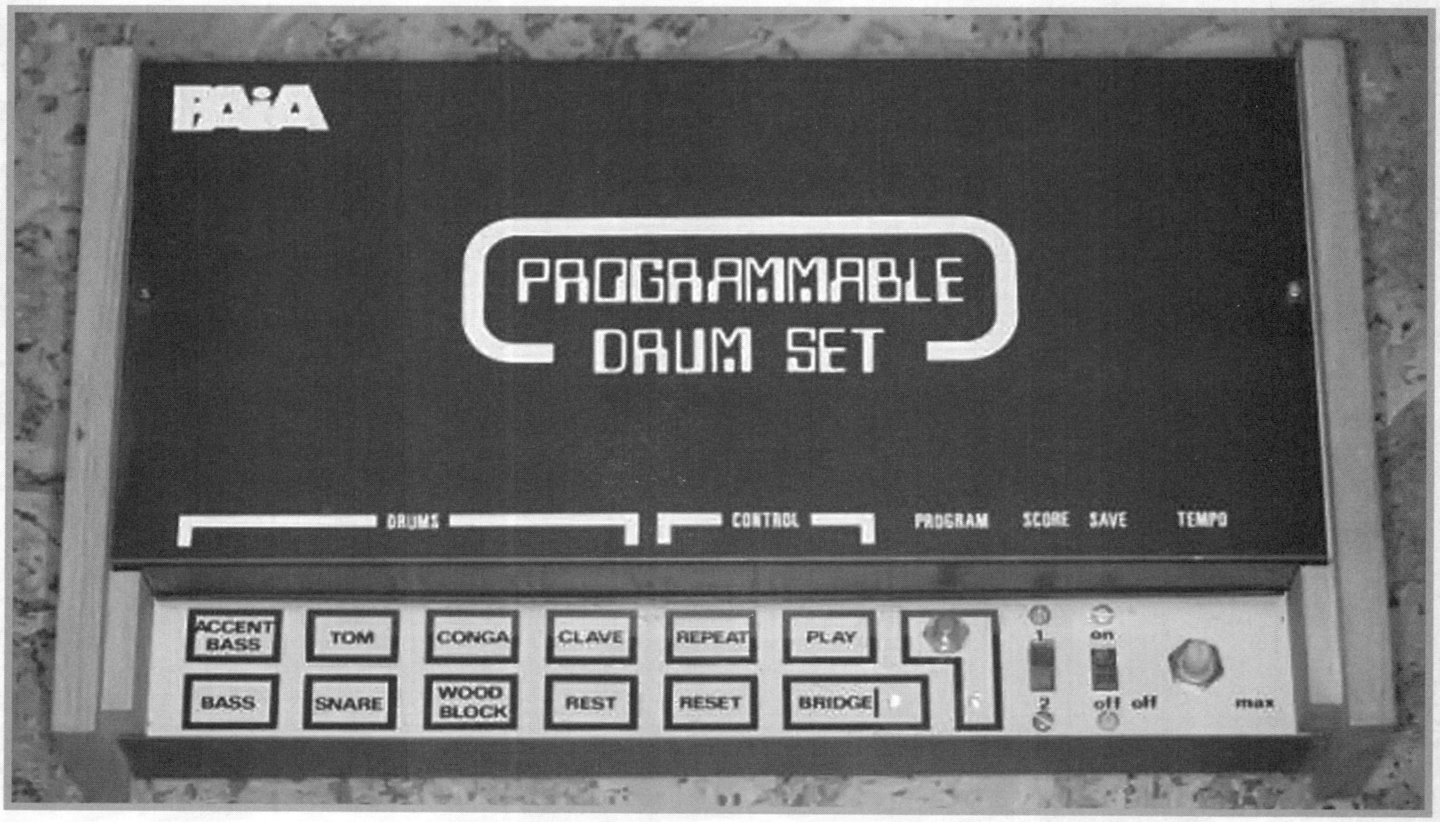

PATTERNS

The 10 Essential Beats

In combining all of the concepts we study on the drums, it is important that we never forget the basics. The basics are the foundation of what makes a great drummer a great musician. This study is what I call "The 10 Essential Beats." No matter what musical situation you're in, whether you have to play, produce, or write, knowing these basic beats, and being able to play anything over them, will definitely aid in getting the job done!

Practice these and also incorporate some of the other concepts in this book and you'll be ready to make good music.

1.

2.

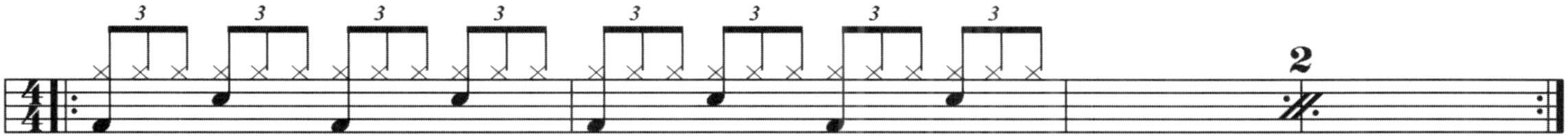

3.

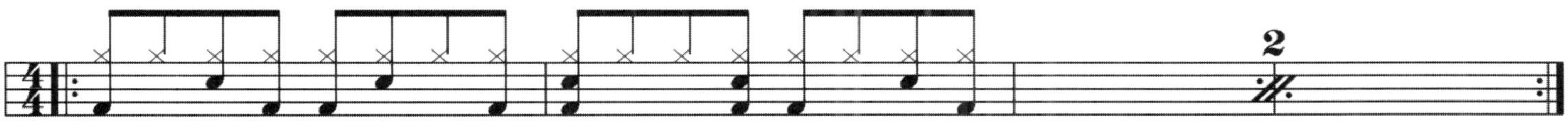

4.

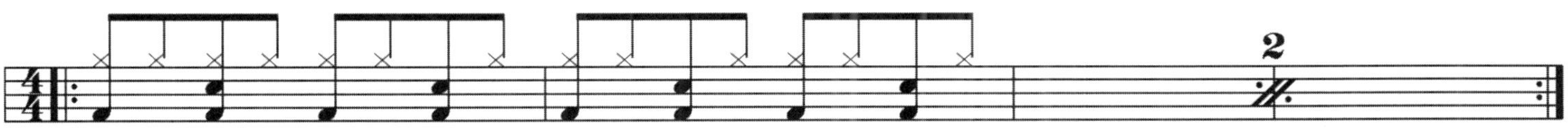

5.

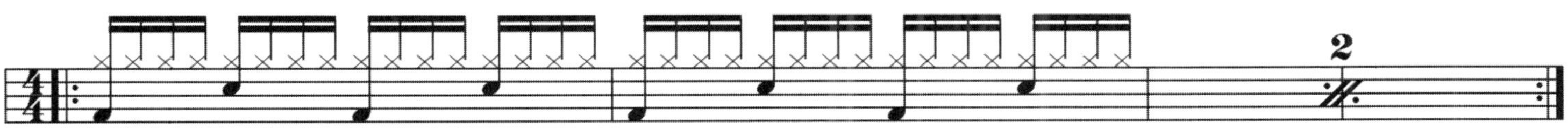

6.

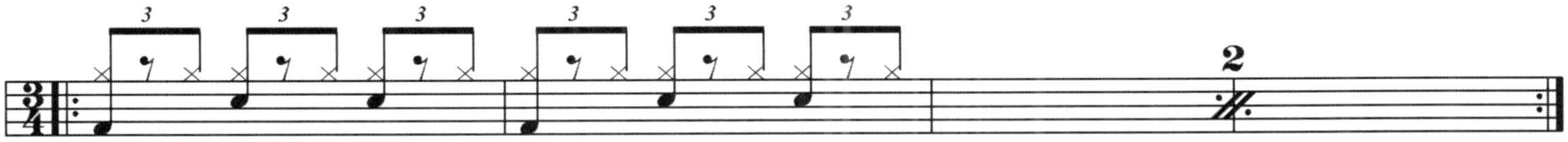

PATTERNS

7.

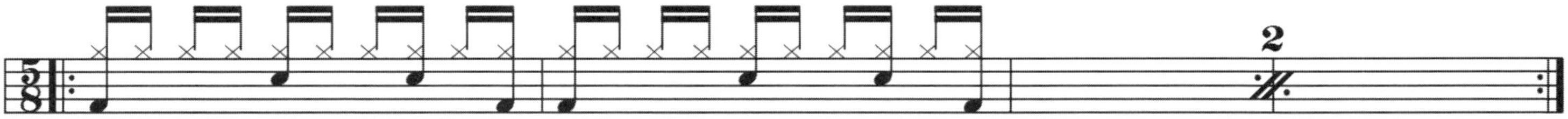

8.

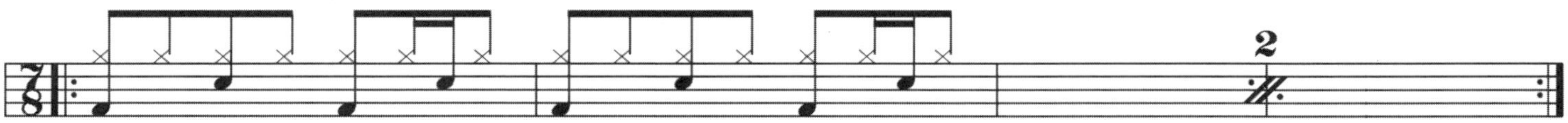

9.

10.

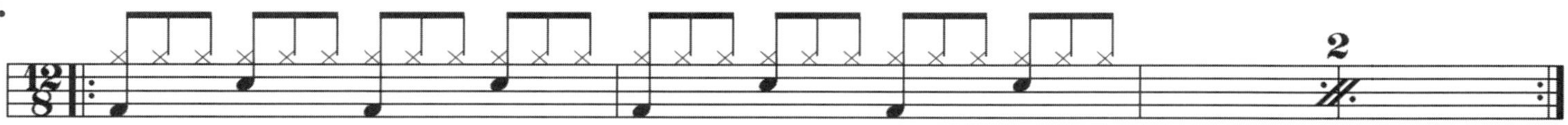

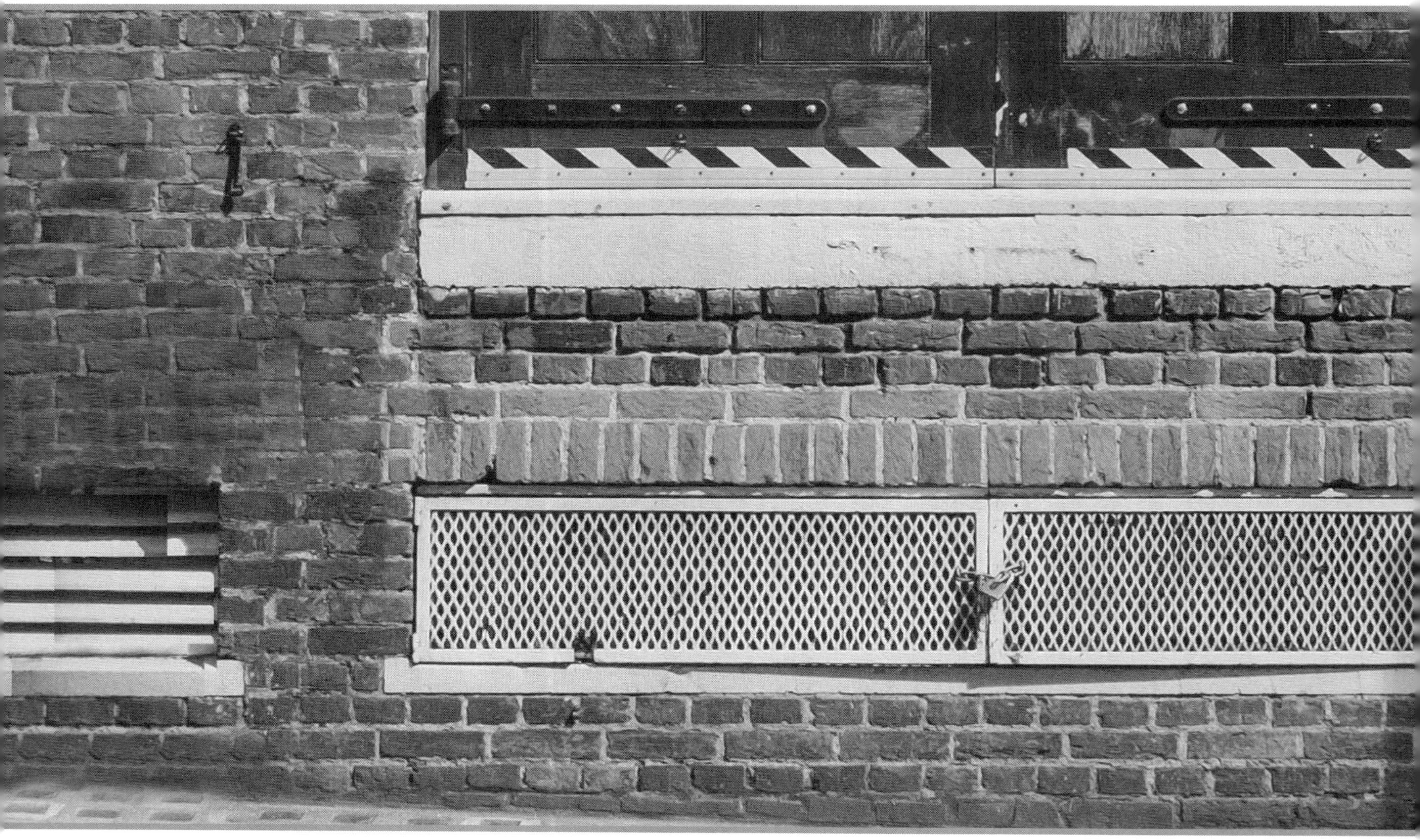

PATTERNS

Study #1

Now we're going to learn something I call "**the point of the head nod.**" The "head nod" is where the beat or pulse lays and is felt the strongest. It is how the beat is meant to move the listener and you. The listener will obviously put their own spin on what's happening, but if done properly the intent can translate more accurately.

Every beat has at least one, if not multiple nod points offering a lot of beat variation and possibilities. The best way to choose a point is to discover the note(s) that creates the most tension and cause the head to want to nod consecutively. I'll show some examples and point out some good options. Note: Anything can alter the point of the head nod from the drums or any other instrument. There are no right or wrong ways to approach this.

33.

34.

choose and play your points with exercises 35-38

35.

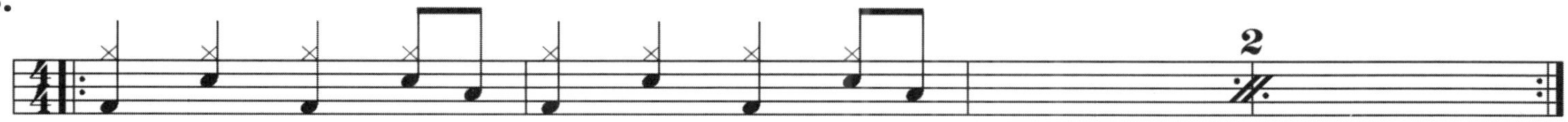

36.

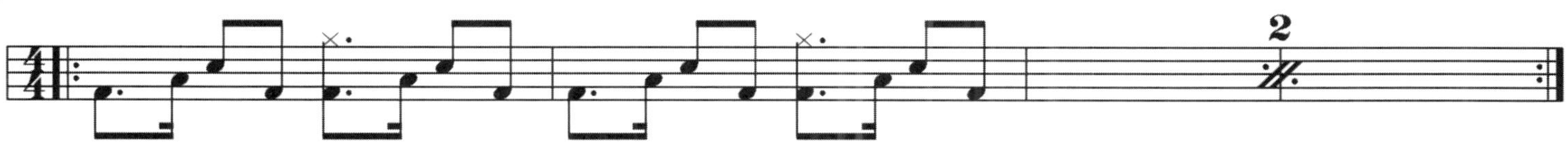

37.

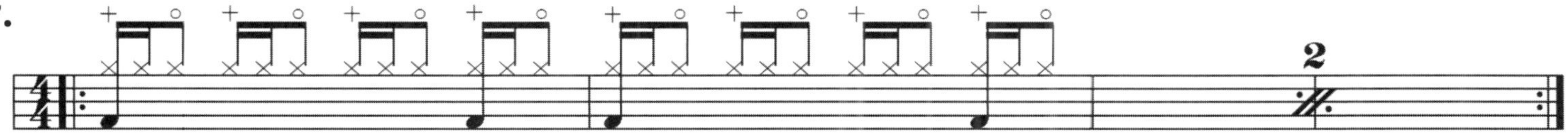

38.

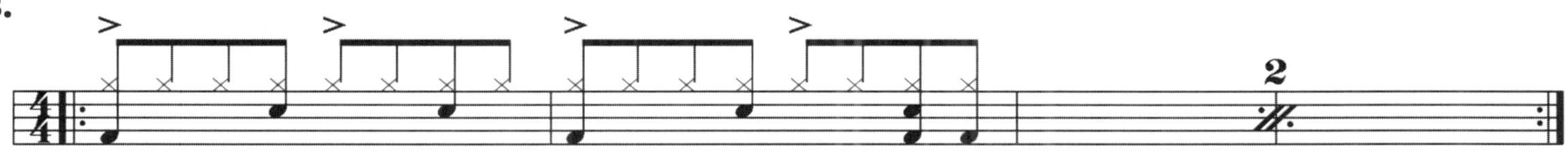

Study #2

Often, a beat is thought of to be kick, snare, and hi-hat or just kick and snare, but any drum can create a beat. Let's explore how we can make any part of the drum into a beat and then combine other drums to make a full beat.

The goal is to be creative. Now what we want to talk about is how to create beats on drums, just different principles that we can use. Here, we're going to create a beat using one drum, and use that theme to create a whole beat using multiple drums.

39.

40.

41.

PATTERNS

42.

ayer 1
ayer 2

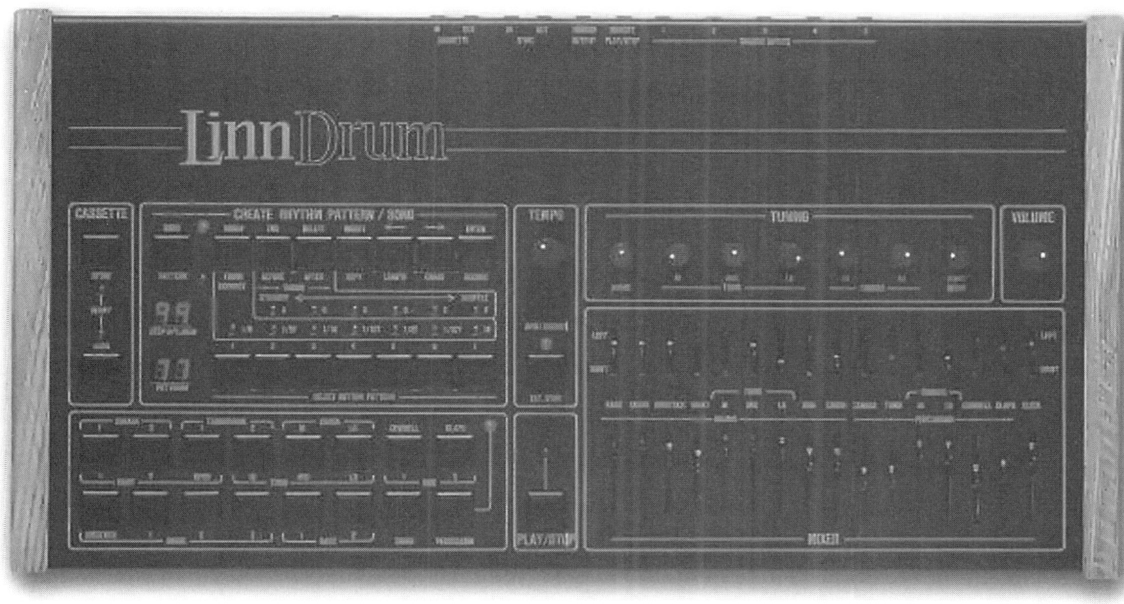
LinnDrum
CASSETTE
CREATE RHYTHM PATTERN / SONG
TEMPO
TUNING
VOLUME
PLAY/STOP
MIXER

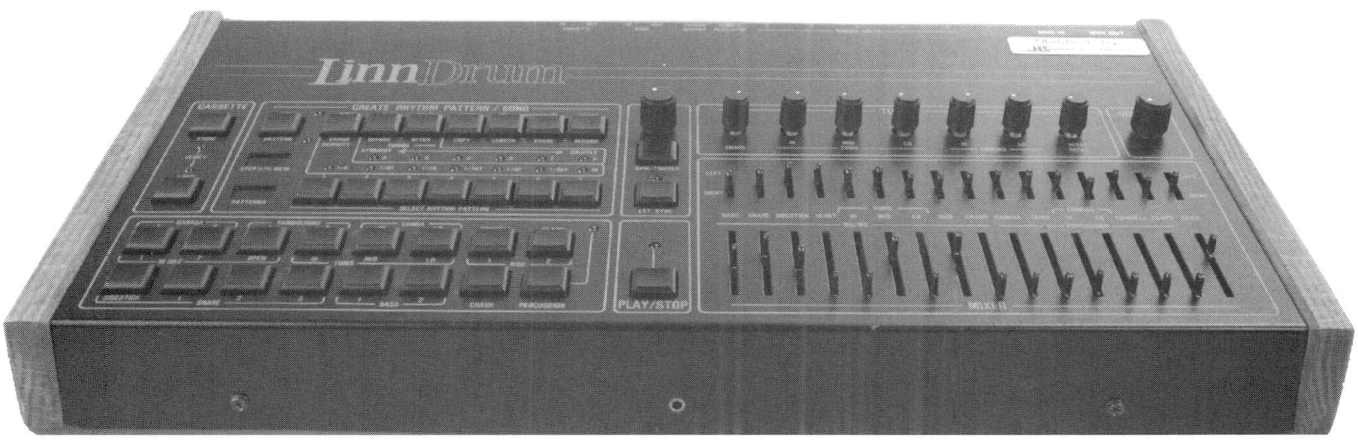
LinnDrum
CASSETTE
CREATE RHYTHM PATTERN / SONG
PLAY/STOP

PATTERNS

Study #3

In this study, we're going to add and subtract notes to create some new ideas. In Study #2, we started with one drum and added notes. Now, what we're going to do is add more notes and then subtract some notes from that. Here are some more exercises to work on that.

43.

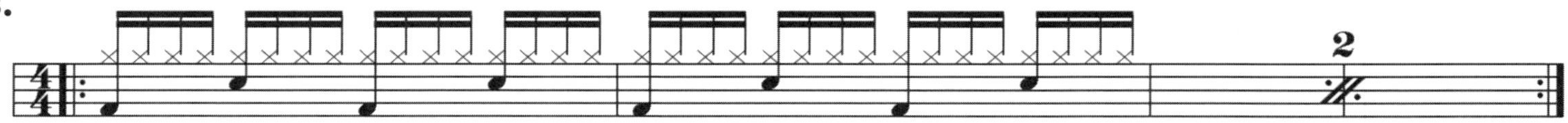

44.

Subtract & Add

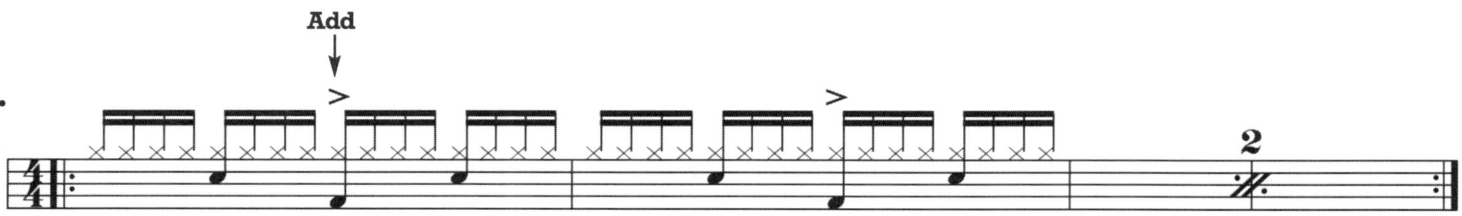

45.

Subtract

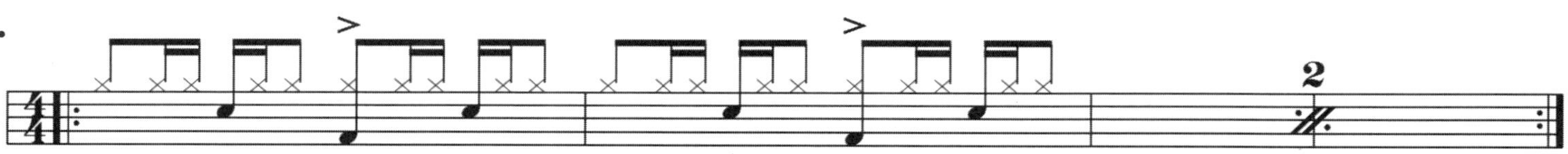

46.

Subtract & Add

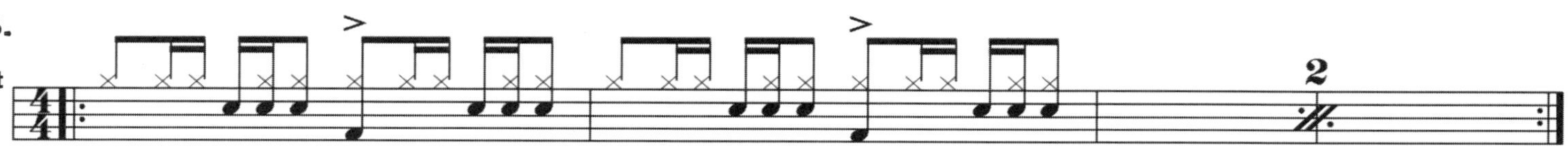

47.

Add

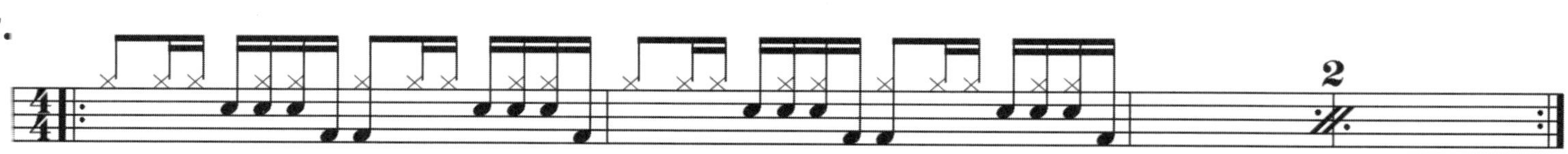

Now let's see how *you* can add & subtract the notes to create a new beat.

48.

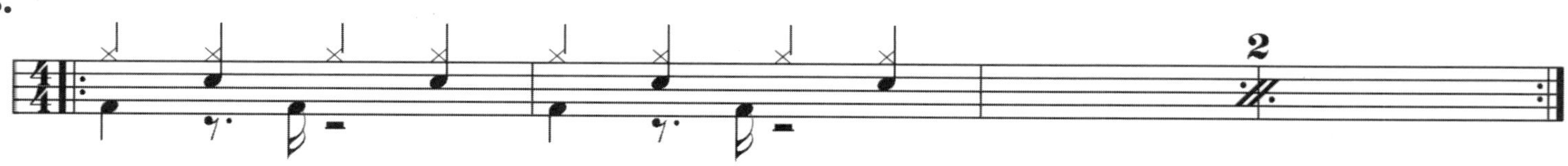

This approach can be used when you're playing live, in the moment. If you're playing and you start thinking this way, you can start coming up with all kinds of different beats on the spot. Or, if you're in the studio, and you're trying to come up with a groove, these methods can help you be very creative.

Study #4

This study takes a look at the concept of **displacement**, which can help create and evolve beats even more. Basically, displacement is moving notes around in a bar. For example, in exercise 50, I displaced the bass drum by a half note, so what was occurring on the kick on beat 1 got moved to beat 3. In exercise 51, the snare drum on beat 2 is displaced by one eighth note. The other exercises continue to move notes around in the bar, creating new, syncopated beats.

49.

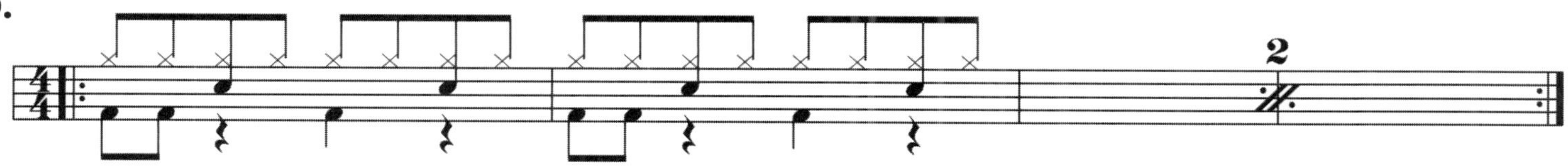

50.

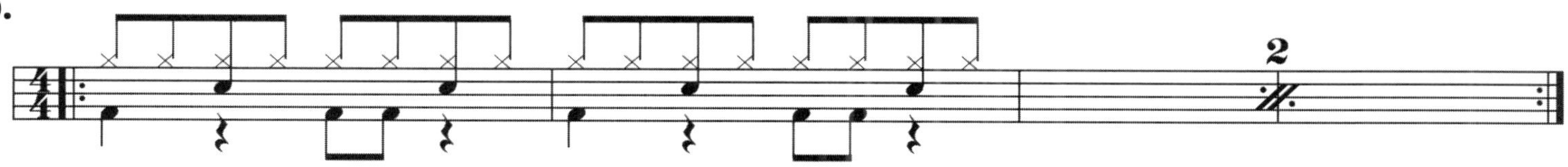

51.

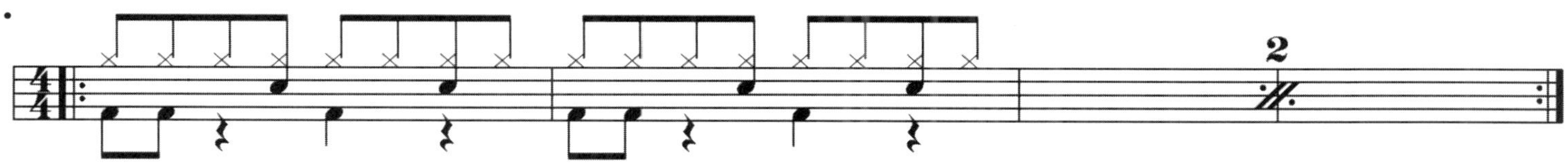

52.

Add

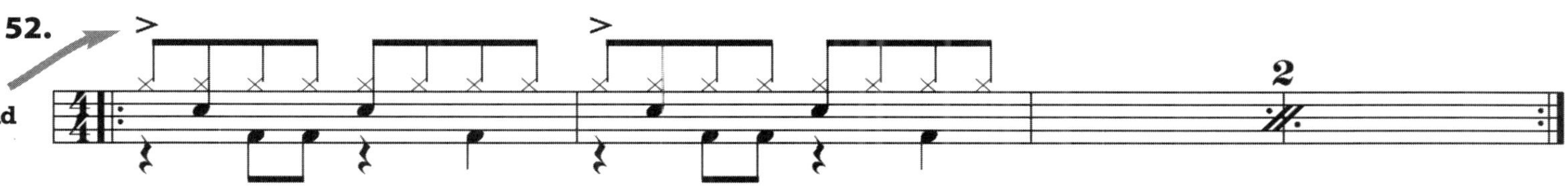

53.

btract & Add

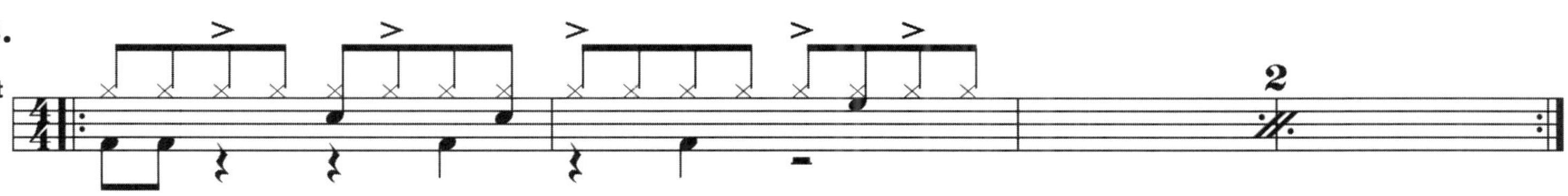

Create your own beat & explore displacement.

54.

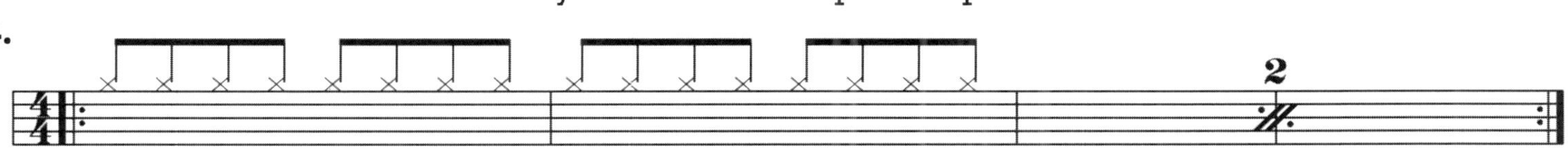

Study #5

Note conversation is an important element to understand with any beat. Let's go over a few methods to hearing this (I call this study Rhythonics). We have a few different ways to approach this:

1. The number/rate concept: Hearing rhythm in numbers and speed.
2. Drum melodics: Hearing rhythm in pitch.
3. Velocity: Hearing rhythmic in dynamics
4. Expression: Hearing rhythm in attitude

Number/Rate

Normally, when people learn drums, they're taught from the standpoint of counting in time, which is very valid, useful, and a great way to approach playing. Now here is a different kind of concept. Instead of having the subdivisions be the focus and the driving piece in counting, here it's more based on the numbers and the speed in which they follow each other.

On the video, I keep the subdivisions, or the time, going between the hi-hat and the kick drum. And, then, I play the number rate concept on the snare. I also improvise with this concept on the video.

55.

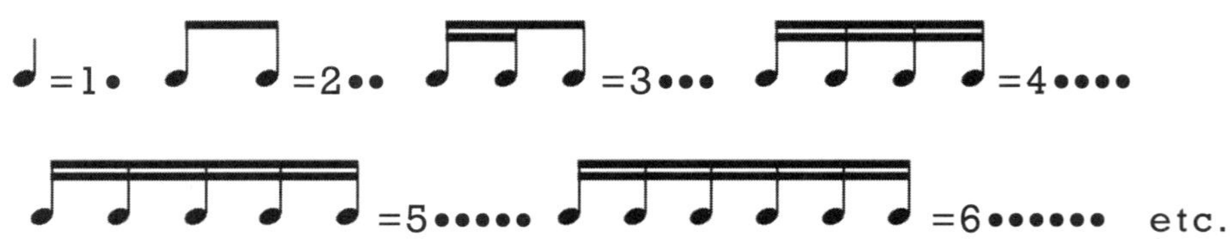

56.

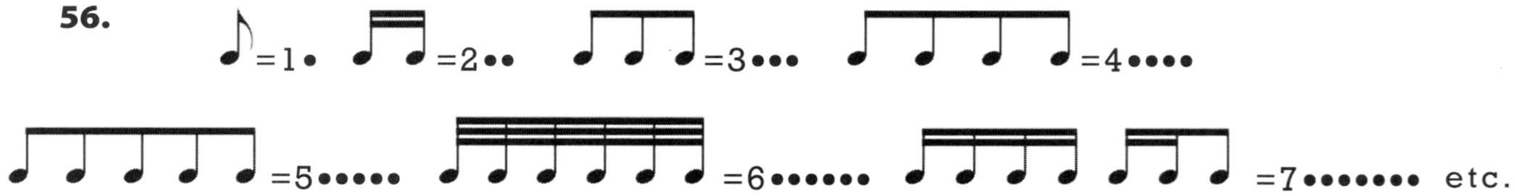

PATTERNS

Drum Melodics

The drums can create melody by the choice of voices. The key is to hear the voice. When I used to listen to drums, I only heard in terms of paradiddles, other rudiments, and how fast or loud something was played. But I didn't hear the actual sounds and sound choices that were made. In these examples, pay attention to sound each drum makes and the patterns involved. There should be a conversation among the sounds you are using.

57.

Velocity

Here I take some eighth notes, and by applying velocity and dynamics, now you have something that's more of a "conversation," something that's telling a story.

58.

PATTERNS

Expression

Expression to me is hearing rhythm in attitude and then playing it. It's not so restricted to hitting notes exactly, or doing things right, or over thinking. It's more so about emotion attitude and feel.

In the video I apply the emotions/expression of "upset," "aggression," "happy," and "sad" to a beat. Try applying expressions to these patterns.

59.

60.

61.

By applying expression, we really start to become musical. When playing music, different moods are expressed. When you don't have lyrics, the instrument can be used to express certain moods. And people can hear that.

Study #6

Drums speak in a different language than other instruments and that's ok. Our primary language is rhythm and what a beautiful language it is. Here are some cadences on the snare, that will help open the ear to hear the language of rhythm better.

Cadence, to me, is about being a lyricist on the drums; playing in a way where it's kind of rhyming and catchy, to make statements on the drums. One of the first cadences I actually ever learned was called "F Troop" and I learned it being a part of a drum corps. I was captivated by it. I demonstrate this cadence on the video. Practice these and see if you can create your own!

62.

63.

64.

Study #7

Here we will use cadence combinations. Try incorporating your own velocity and expression to diversify the communication of beats.

65.

66.

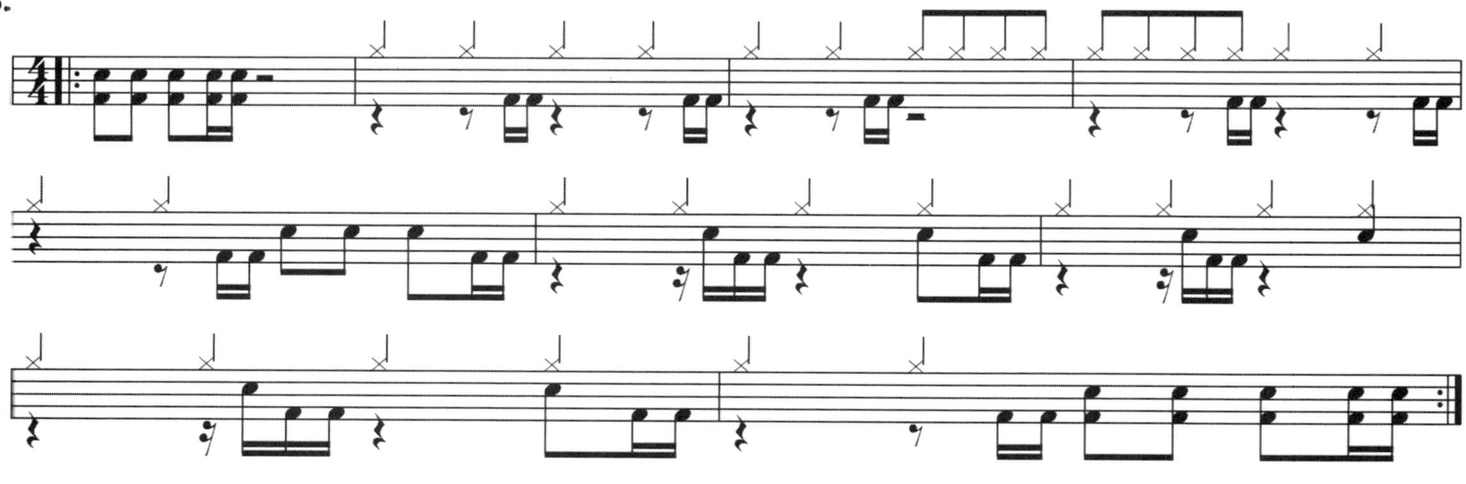

PATTERNS

67.

PATTERNS

Study #8

Now let's explore some more cadences with all four concepts around the kit. Here are a few that will help to open up your playing.

68.

69.

PATTERNS

70.

SONICS

Sonics are about the sound each individual drum makes. Any drum is capable of an infinite amount of sounds, but each sound has its own character and feel. So, what we want to do is explore the sounds of the drums and then practice taking those sounds, placing them in a beat, and then change the register of each drum to see how it impacts the feel and mood.

One thing I've learned from playing drums and producing is that each part of the drums has a character that can change into a variety of moods. Choosing the sounds that will create the feeling desired and has everything to do with what the beat or song is. We will discuss some of those different qualities and show how it can affect the way you play (as well as the way other musicians play!).

"You play what you hear."

Study #9

Each drum has a unique note register where it sits, but as we tune a drum that register can change. It's important to also know that the sonic concept is not limited just to the drums, but also includes your technique, room, and other variables. Our lane is wide open with possibilities. How we approach sonics will open up our musical creativity. Obviously, there are an infinite amount of drums and tones, but here is a basic list to start.

- Cymbal bell: Very high range
- Cymbals: Medium to high range, stands out
- Hi-hat: Medium to high range, sharp cut
- Rim shot: High range, very sharp cut
- High snare: High range, cuts
- Mid snare: Mid range, balanced
- Deep snare: Mid/low, comfortable pocket
- High tom: Mid to high range, medium cut
- Mid tom: Medium warm, balanced
- Low tom: Low in nature, bold
- Bass drum: Very warm, full of support

Here is a beat that I often use when sound checking to hear my sound. Let's see what happens when we change the registers with in the beat.

SOUND CHECK PATTERN

71.

VARIATIONS

72.

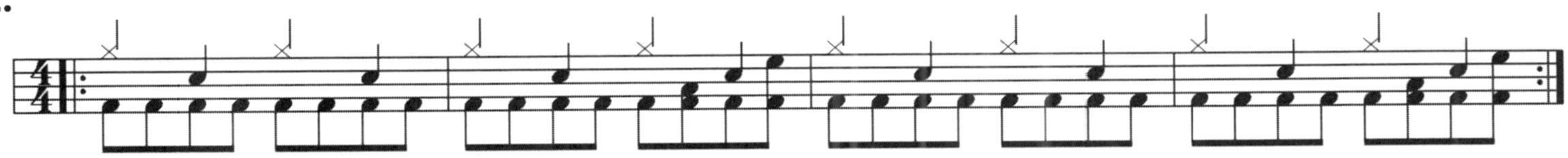

73.

74.

Study #10

Tempo and sonics go hand in hand. Sometimes if you change the tempo, the sonics may need to change as well, because of the new mood that has been created. Being acquainted with sound and tempo will help you know how to create the right mood. Try these examples fast, then slow them down and change the registers to hear the difference. This ear training will aid in your decision-making on choosing the right sound for any situation.

75.

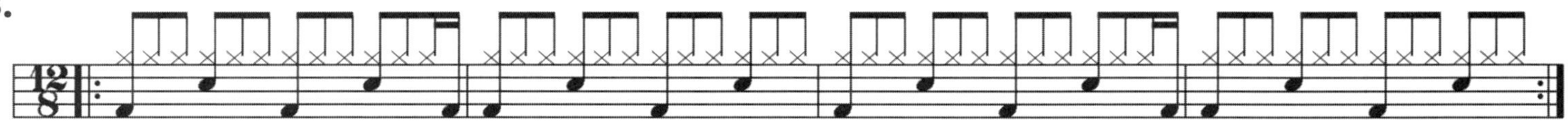

76.

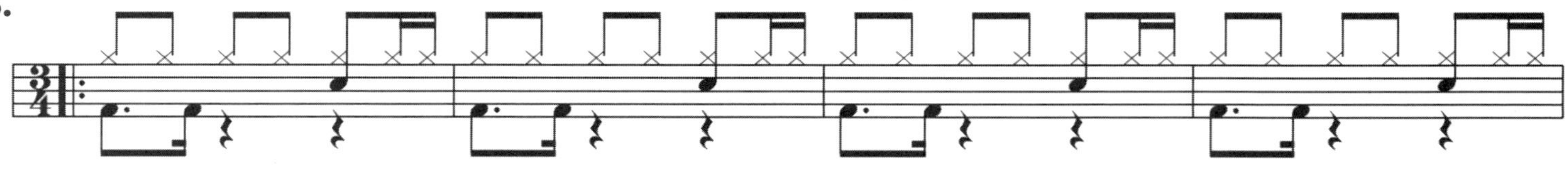

77.

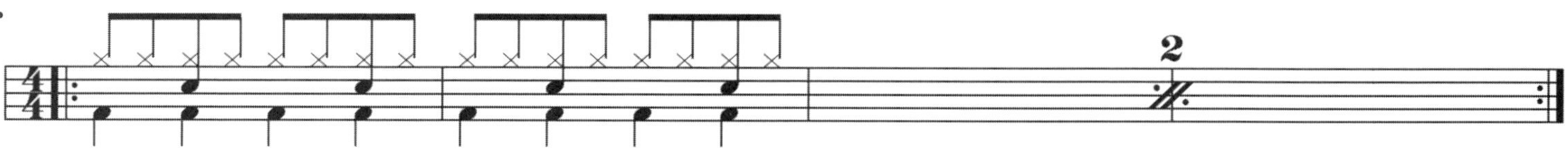

78.

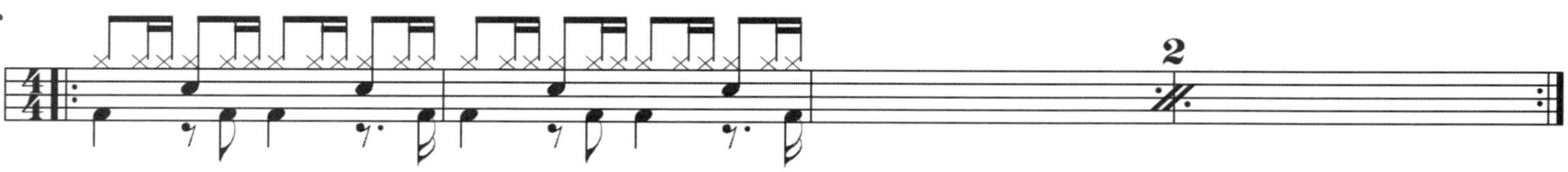

Study #11

Sonic creativity: I have taken one beat and created several beats by slowing the tempo down and changing the registers. We'll also incorporate some addition and subtraction of notes to expand our creativity. Practice these to further develop your ear.

79.

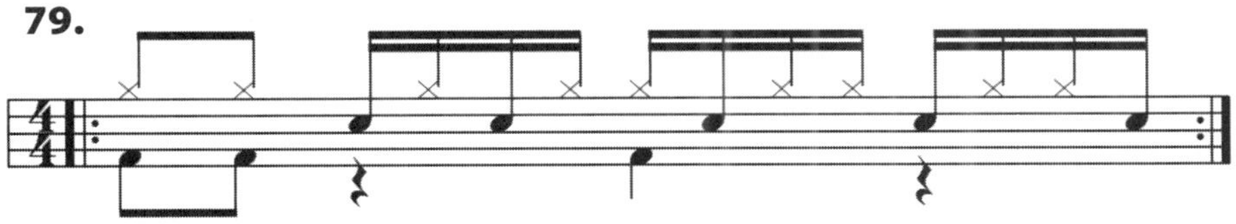

80.

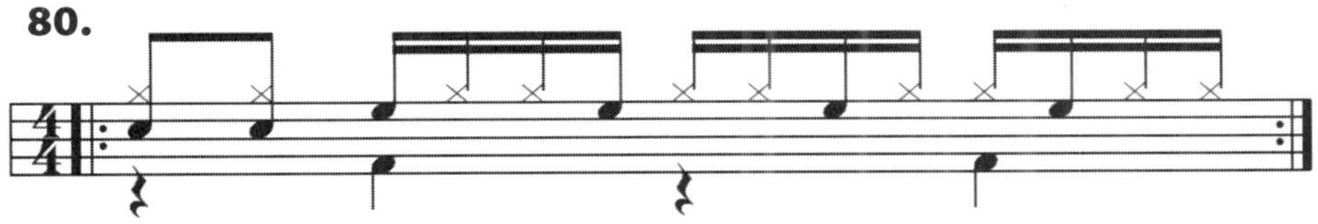

81.

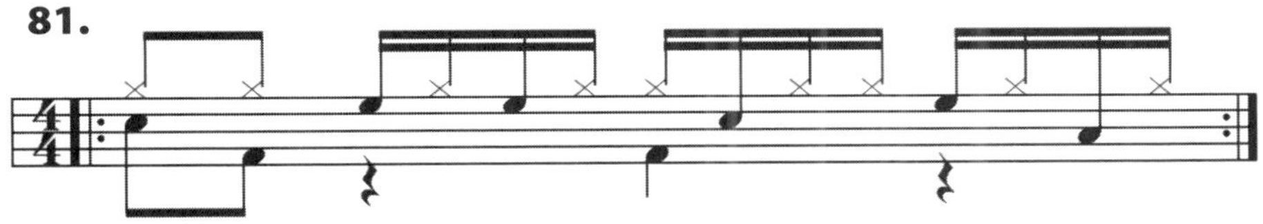

82.

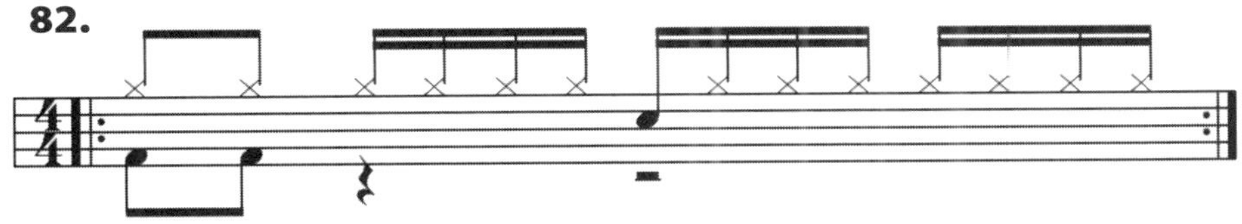

83.

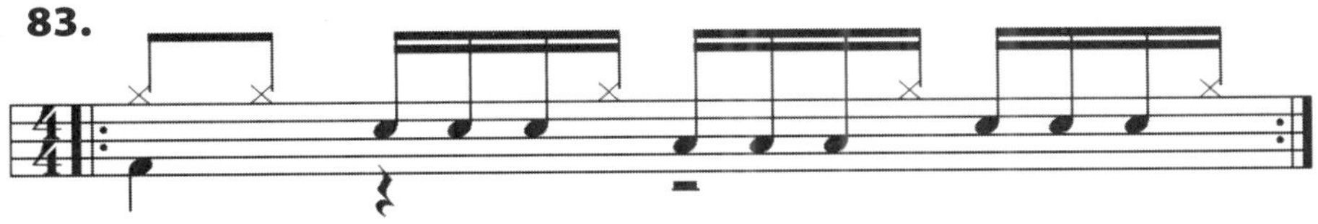

84.

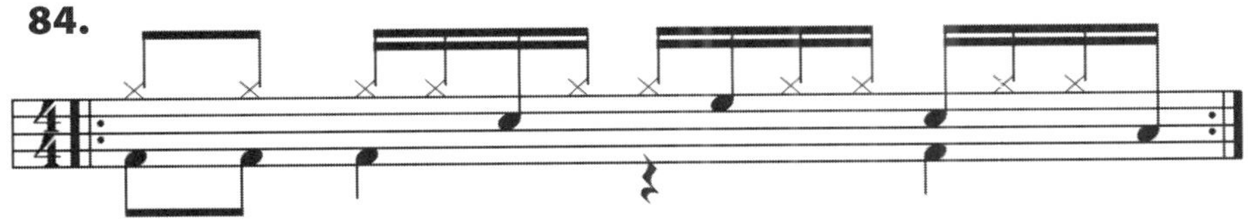

85.

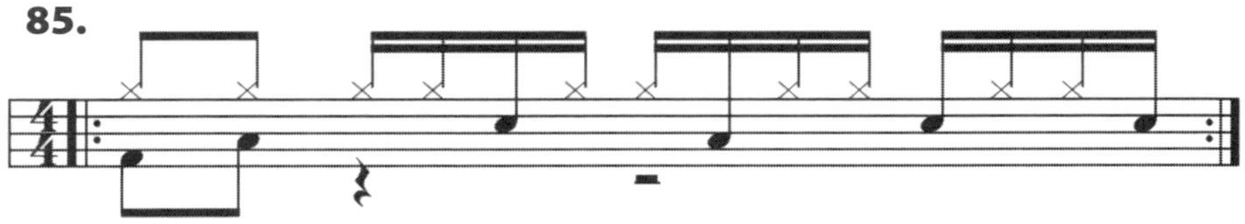

86.

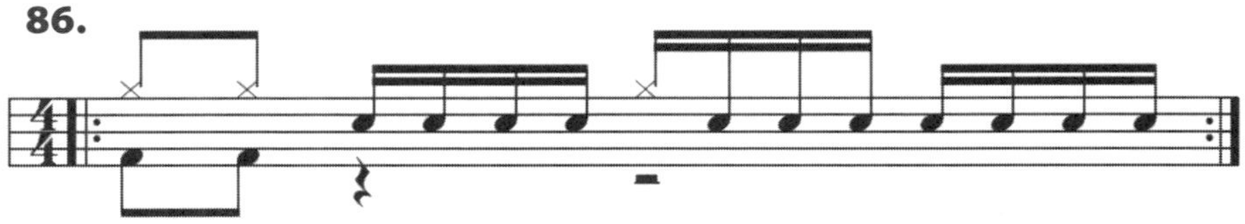

87.

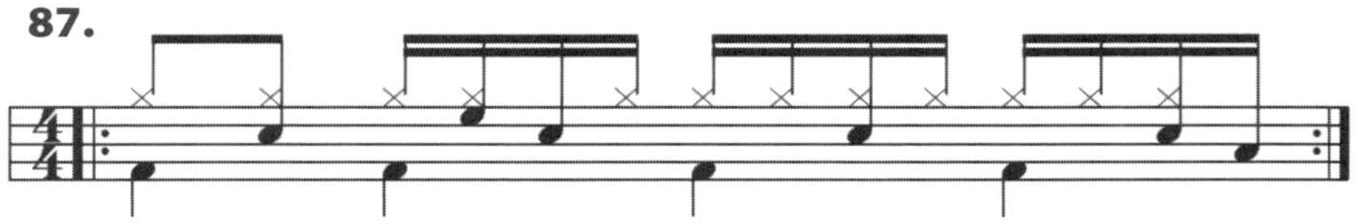

88.

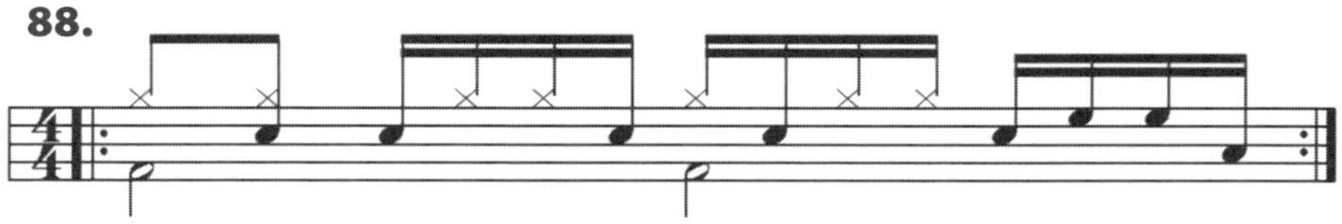

SONICS

Study #12

There are many ways to approach sonics on the drums to be creative. Another way is to imagine the register that you are playing in is another whole instrument. I will give some examples and let's see how your creativity expands.

16th-note shaker

89.

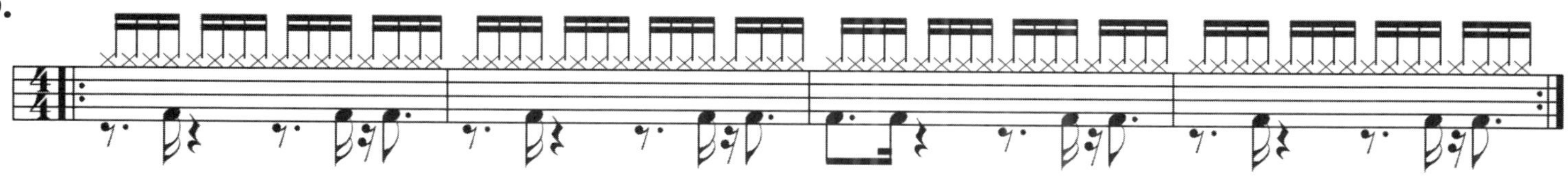

the rim shot bongo snare

90.

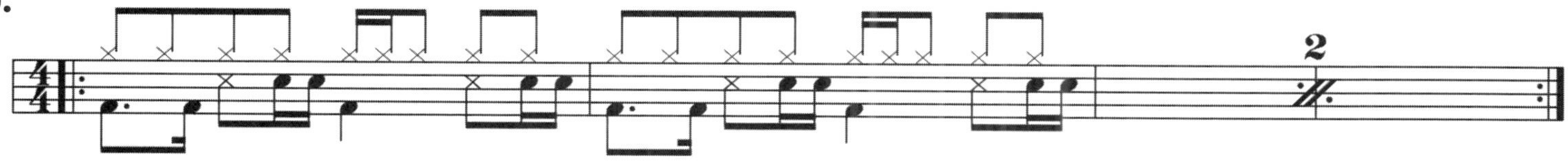

the hand clap stack & snare

91.

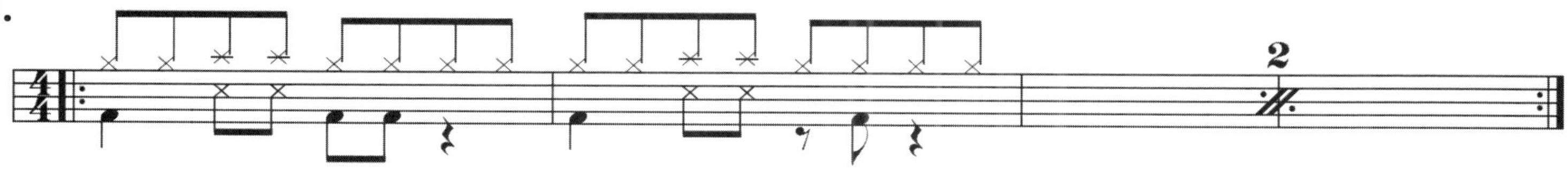

the 808 cymbal groove

92.

What do you hear with these rhythms?

93.

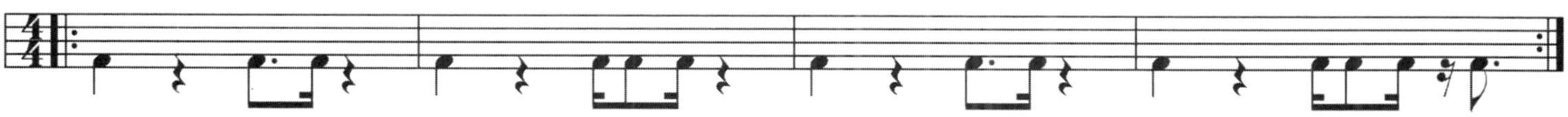

94.

95.

SONICS

Study #13 (The Loops and Sample Section)

Mixing electronics with acoustic drums widens the range of possibilities.

- Constant: Playing pad as a constant sound and varying the acoustic sounds around it.
- Two to One: At least two electronic sounds to one acoustic sound.
- Playing pad as an auxiliary percussion instrument.
- The Loop: Playing like a loop.

Note: For the examples that include an electric pad, try using a hand clap sound. If you don't have an electronic pad, imagine your acoustic drums as electronic to create the sounds as best as you can.

Constant

96.

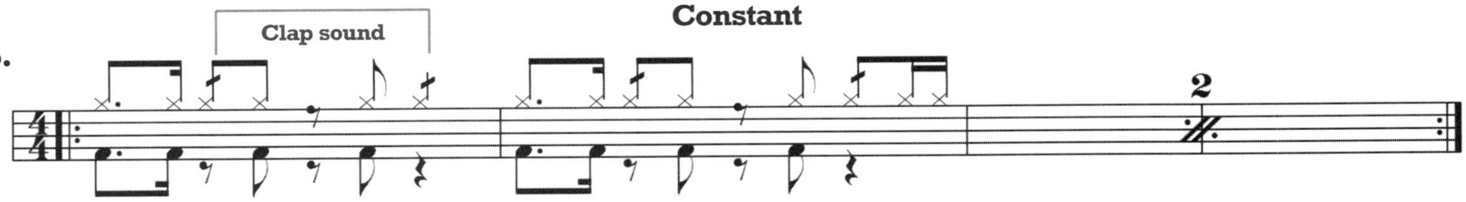

Two to One

97.

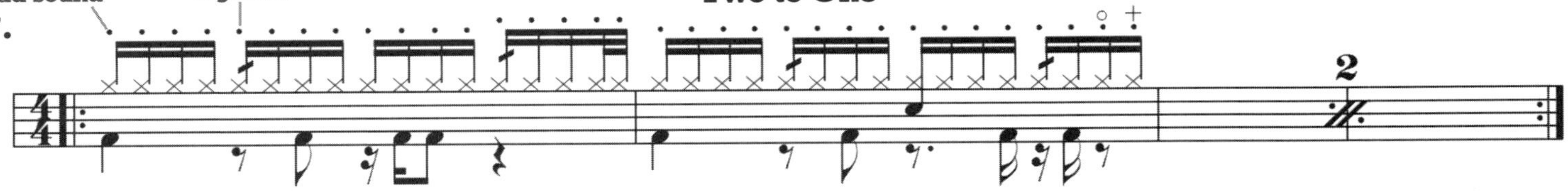

98.

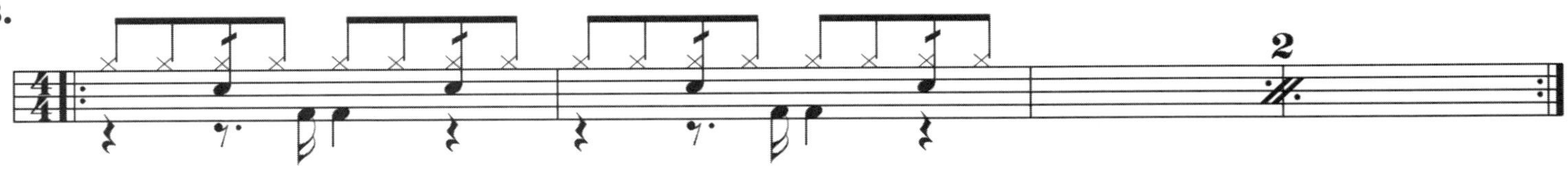

99.

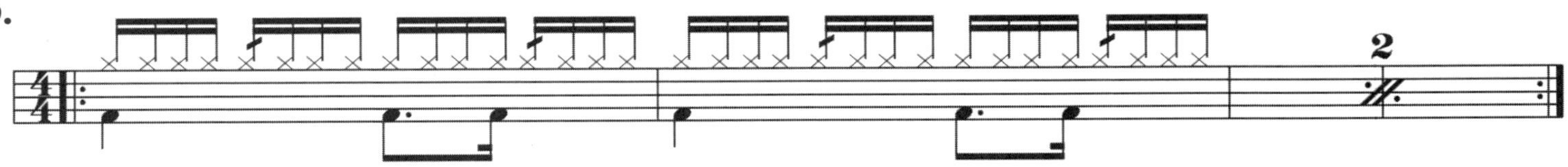

Percussive

100.

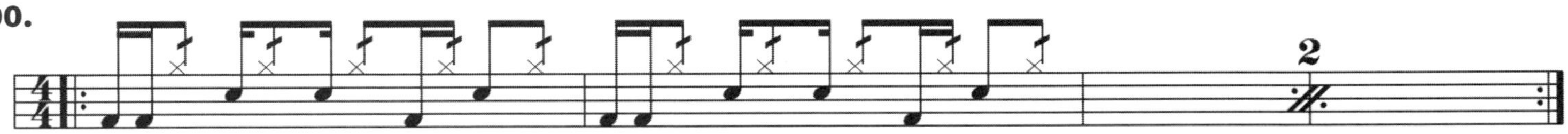

The Loop

101.

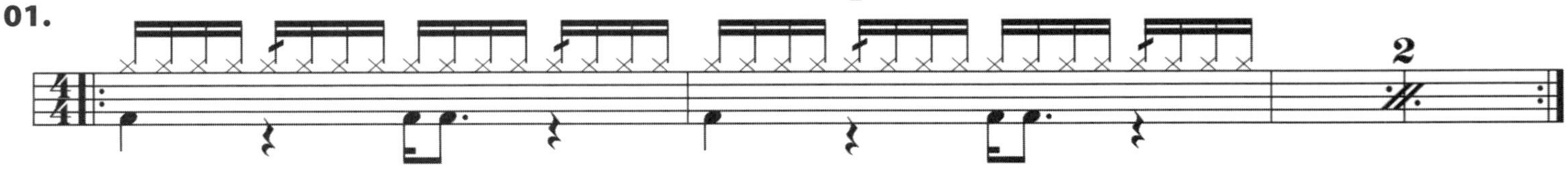

MUSICAL SWAG

Most people can't technically tell why they liked something, but they can describe how it made them feel. It's the way you play and how you feel about what you play. This isn't so focused on the notes and "getting it right," but more concerned about how it feels and how your energy is projecting. I learned this concept by listening to different producers, but one of the main producers that I really keyed in on was again J Dilla.

Dilla seemed to care more about how it felt—and if it felt right, then it was right. He also listened to a lot of different genres of music and respected them all. So what he was able to do was hear a different genre of music and put his thing on it.

On the video, I take a songo groove and demonstrate how to turn it into a hip-hop beat, using this kind of approach. What I want to show here is how to take another genre of music, play the part, and then put that genre of music into another vibe, whatever your vibe is, and turn it into a beat.

"Sometimes the feeling can be heard more than the actual notes."

Musical swag is my term for the unique way someone can make the music feel. So there's personal swag and musical swag. This is a very underrated but important topic for any player and is determined by many factors. Understanding how to create the right feel or swag, just like everything else, is a lifelong study, but the rewards for understanding how it works are immediate.

The "Dilla Style"

A lot of people have talked about by Dilla's approach, and most times, they point to the drums, specifically that the drums are either behind or ahead of the beat. The thing to know is that in a live or studio setting the other band members can either behind or ahead of the beat. This is certainly a part of it. What I would like to bring to the forefront is that the concept really had more to do with just being organic and playing music than anything else. Dilla incorporated a lot of different kinds of music, as you can hear in all the different kinds of samples that he used. Many times, because he was taking a pre-recorded sample of live musicians, and putting those live musicians with technology to try to create a feel, a "push and pull effect" was naturally created.

In listening to his music I could tell that in order to get the right feel, he would have to speed up the snare or slow down the kick—he was trying to get the right feel based on what he had to work with. I think that because it worked so well, it's turned into a misconception, where to play the "Dilla" style is to either be behind the beat or ahead of the beat. What is important is playing the music keeping a strong beat, playing the style, and playing with conviction. On the video I discuss and demonstrate this further, including practicing with a click. Keep in mind that whether you are ahead or behind the click isn't necessarily the major focus when learning this style.

MUSICAL SWAG

Study #14

Here we will get to the core of what this vibe is about. One of the most misunderstood concepts is that in a band setting the drums = the beat. This is not necessarily accurate.

"Every musical instrument working together = the beat."

When this is understood it provides the proper approach, whether composing, playing in a band, or playing a solo. We will outline various rhythms to show how to change them into hip-hop beats.

These are examples of essential styles that all drummers should know. All of these styles have elements that can be fused with other ideas to create beats.

BEMBE/BEAT

102.

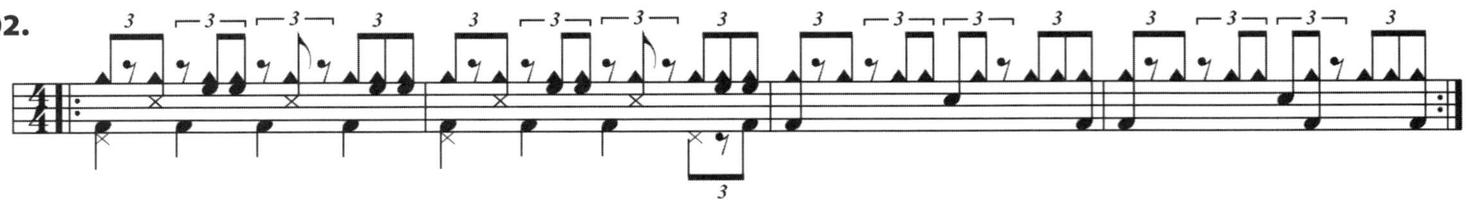

SONGO/BEAT

103.

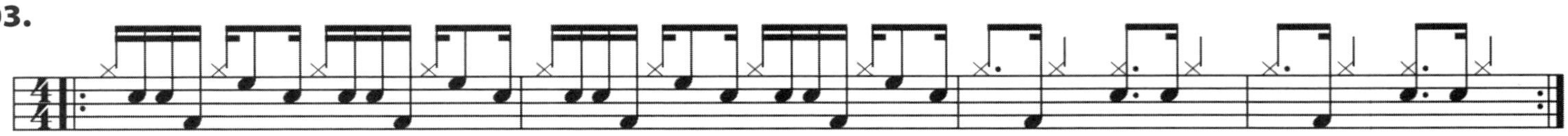

SAMBA/BEAT

104.

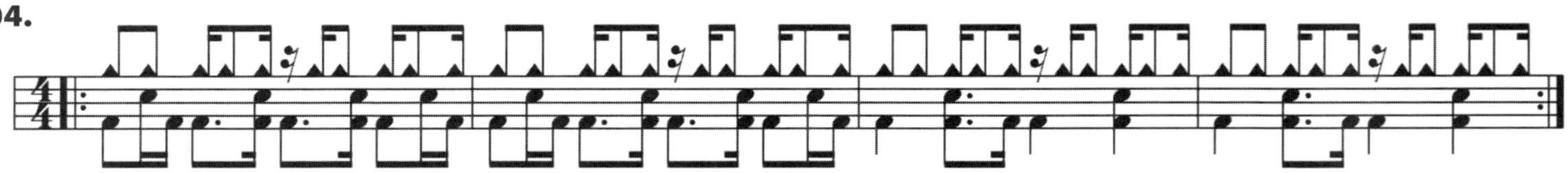

SHUFFLE/BEAT

105.

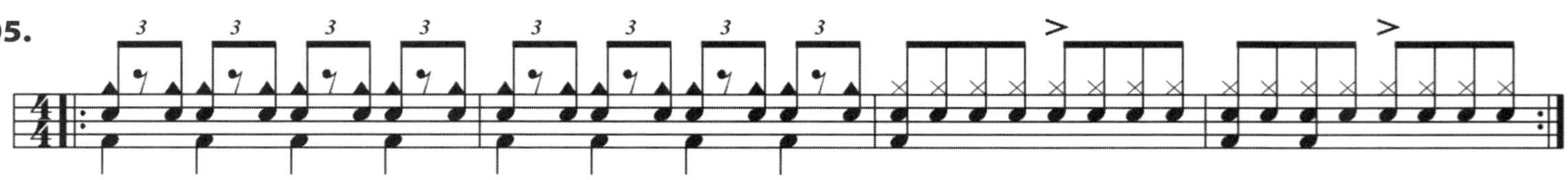

SWING/BEAT

106.

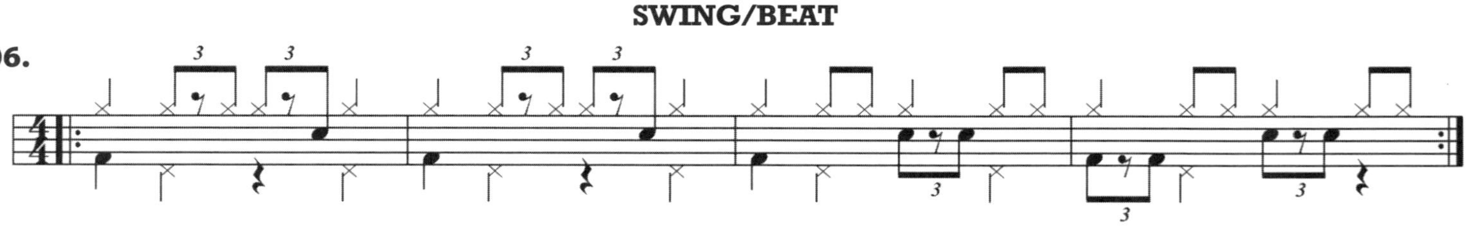

MUSICAL SWAG

Study #15

Here we have some exercises that are designed for practice with the click. Try playing these ahead of the beat, behind the beat, and on the beat.

107.

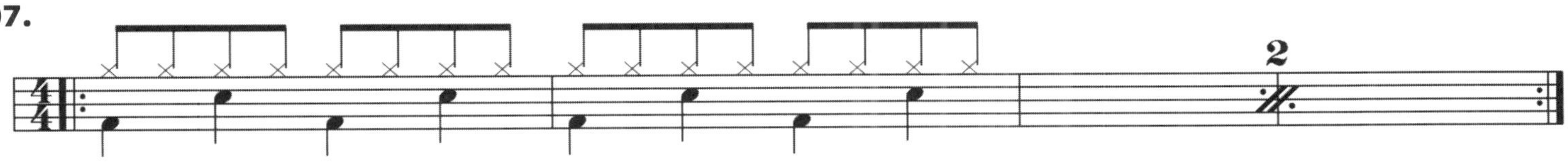

108.

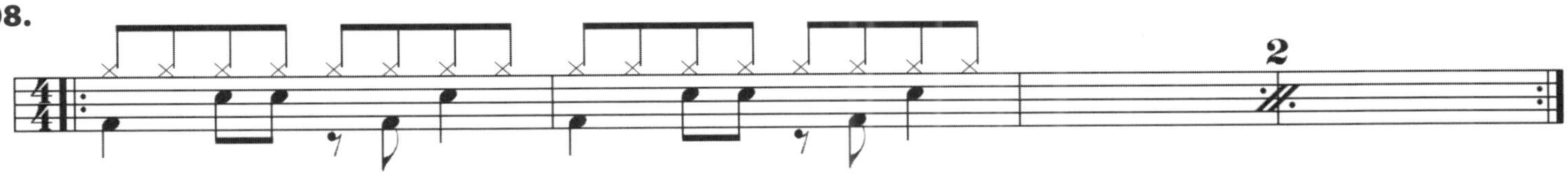

109.

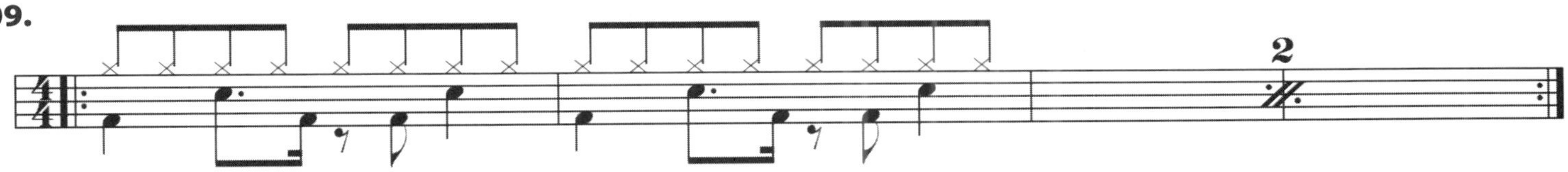

110.

111.

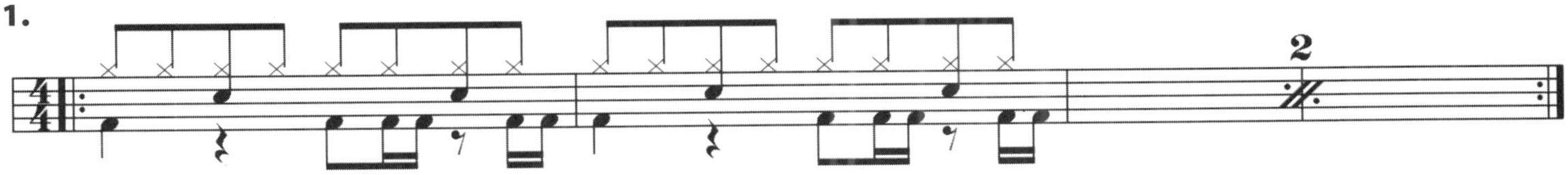

112.

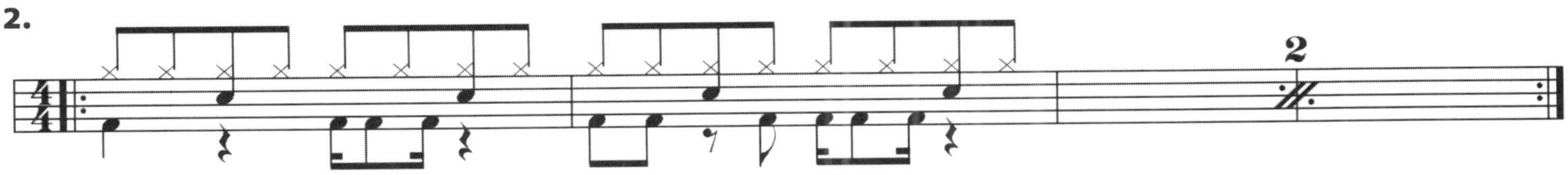

113.

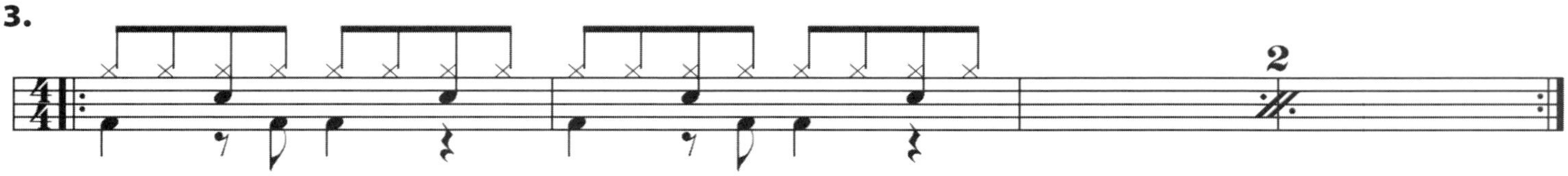

114.

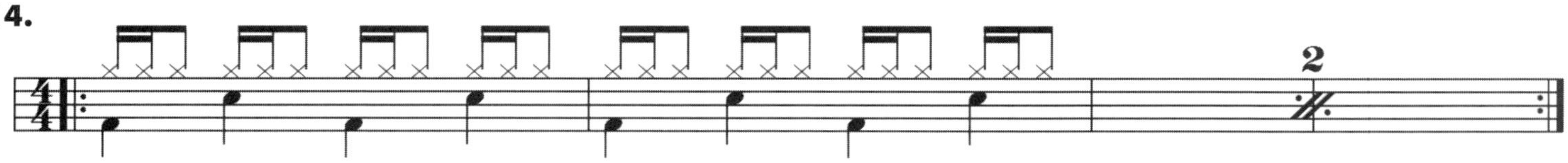

115.

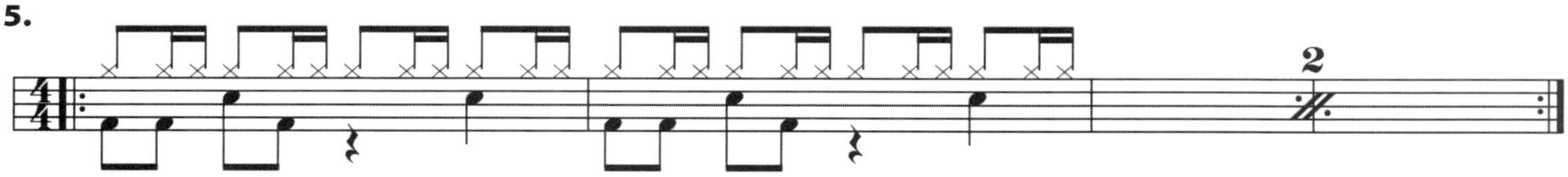

116.

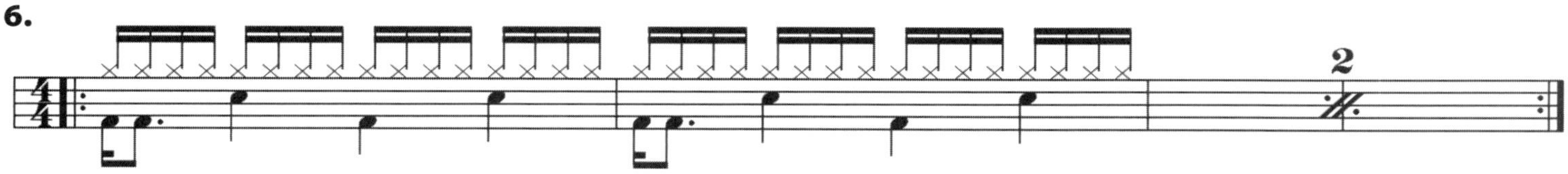

117.

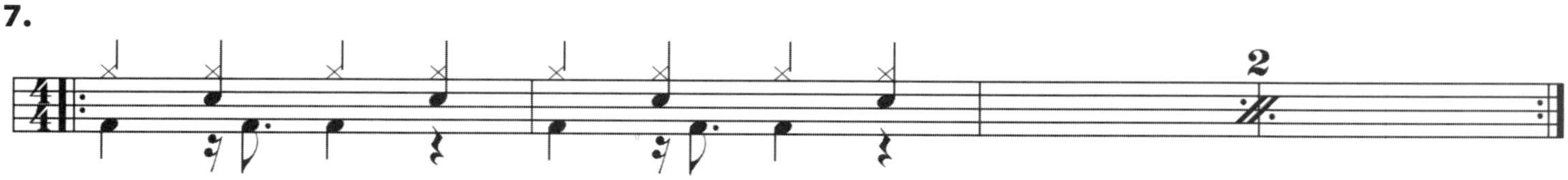

MUSICAL SWAG

Study #16

This study is designed to be played without a click. They should feel organic but still be played with good time. When the hi-hat pattern stops, the goal is to not lose the beat.

118.

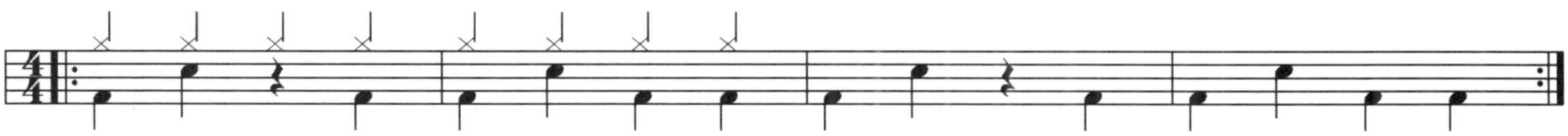

119.

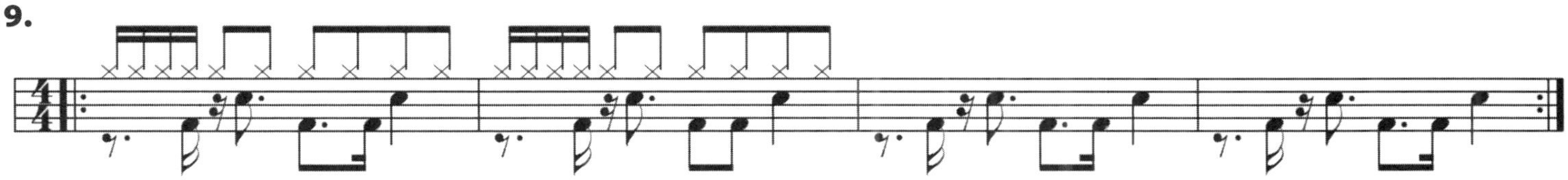

120.

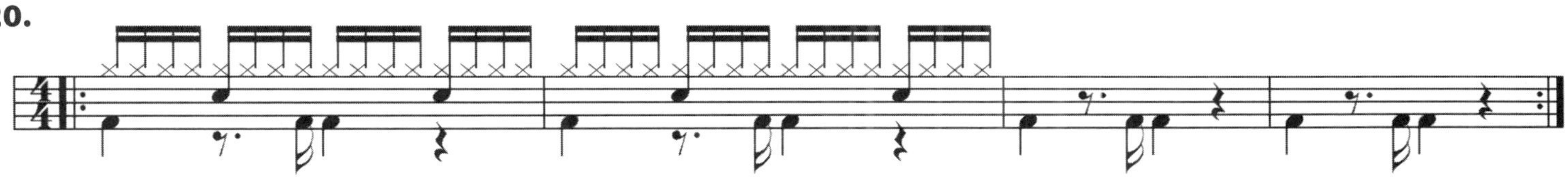

121.

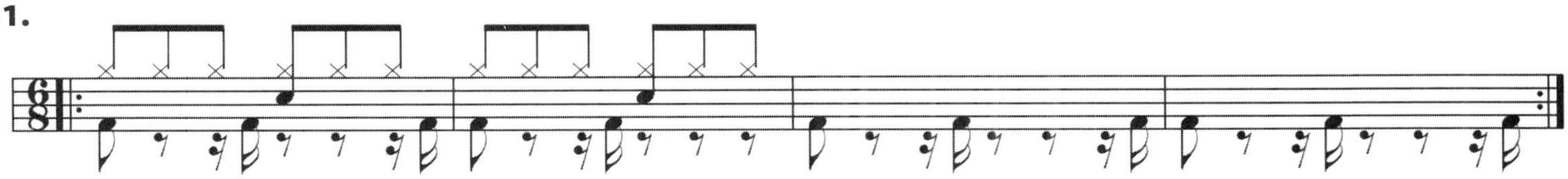

Study #17

These examples are designed for you to focus on tempo. Try these beats at a variety of different speeds while still keeping a solid feel.

122.

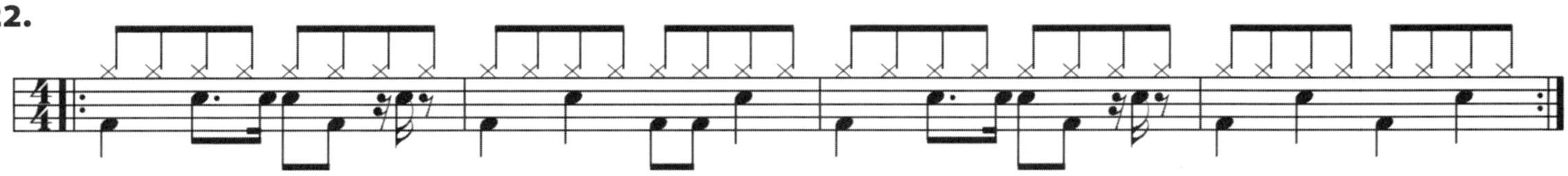

123.

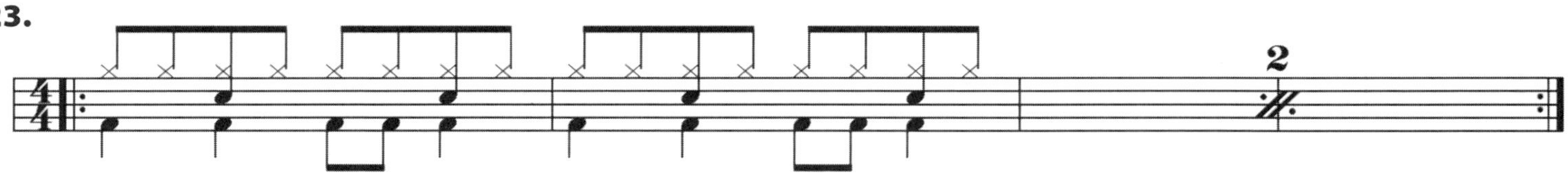

124.

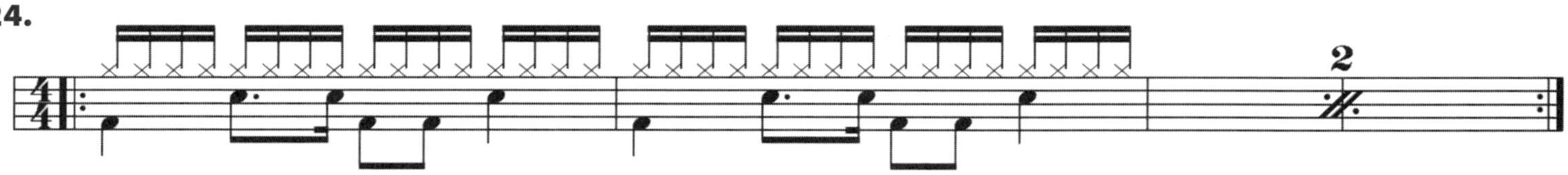

125.

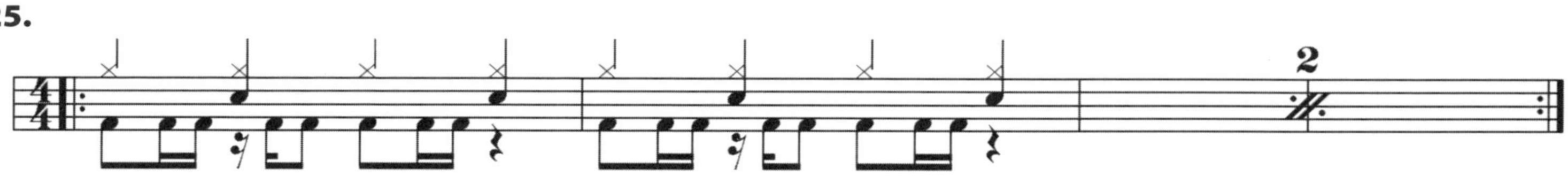

126.

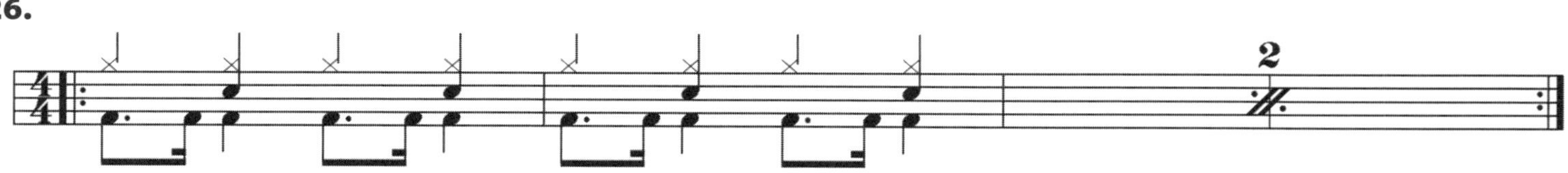

PERFORMANCE

Whether in the studio or live, having a good performance is based on many factors. It is the full summary of all that has been practiced and rehearsed. It also has elements that most drummers may experience but are not sure of what's actually happening. This part is really intricate, but it can really connect you to the music, other musicians and the audience.

Study #18

Whether performing in the studio or at a live concert, knowing how to approach playing a song is vitally important. We will go over some of the concepts I've learned from playing and producing.

Music Motion

As soon as the downbeat of a song or groove is played, that initial beat creates a motion. What you would need to understand is the flow of that motion, and how to navigate through it. It can be a situation where it's not easy to pinpoint what's happening with the motion based on who you're playing with. For instance, if you're playing with a bass player and they're pushing one way, but you know the song should go another way, there can be confusion as to the motion. The drums rhythmically articulates like no other instrument, so being sure and in sync with the musical director will help cut out confusion.

Motion Control

In any musical situation there's push and pull and motion that happens. There are things that you can do to establish where the motion should be and keep it there. On the video I play a basic pattern and demonstrate how putting accents in different parts of the beat can give a sense of where the feel is.

Tempo

In keeping with the "motion" concept, the next area is tempo. In a performance setting, the tempo has a lot to do with the motion that you're trying to convey and keep locked in. Establishing tempo at the beginning of song can happen a few ways. A lot of times, we are expected to be the keepers of the time, including counting off the song. Sometimes, the bandleader may count in, or the singer may count it off. The idea is there needs to be some kind of trust where, if someone else is counting off the tempo for you, either they know the right tempo, or when you take it over, you know the right tempo. When this happens, and there's a trust, then that makes it easier to apply some of these concepts of keeping the motion.

On the video I demonstrate some sixteenth-note patterns and apply the concepts of motion.

PERFORMANCE

How to Move the Music: Hi-Hat Patterns, Anticipations, Accents

All of these things help to shape the groove and motion. Check out the video for this section to see some more demonstrations.

127.

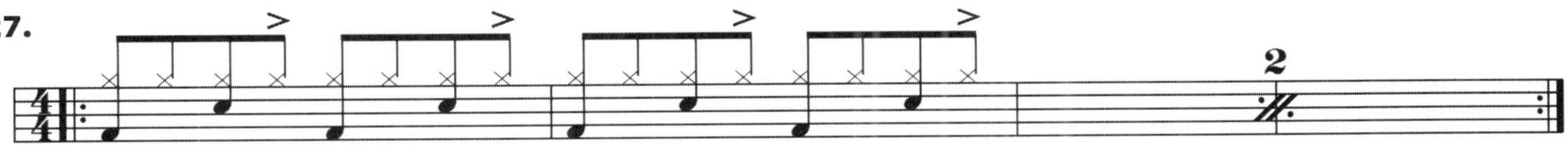

128.

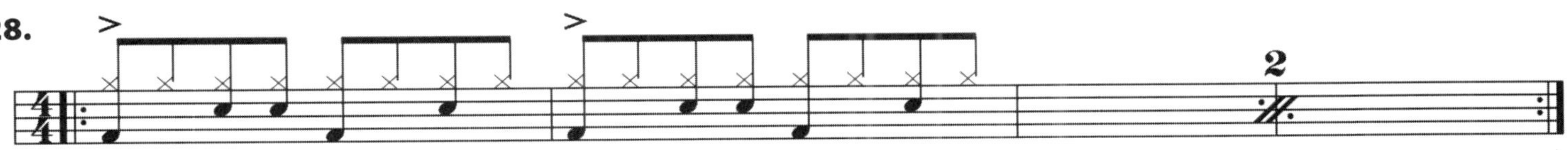

129.

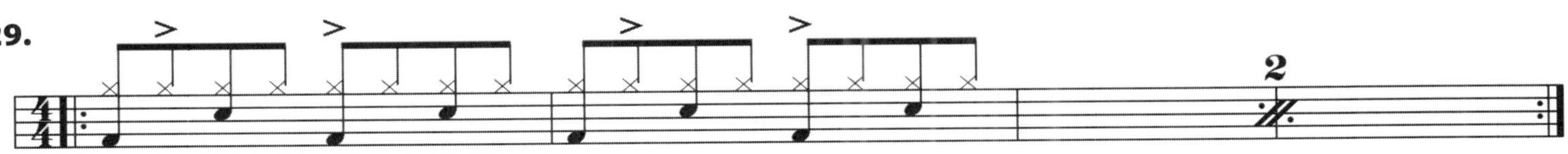

130.

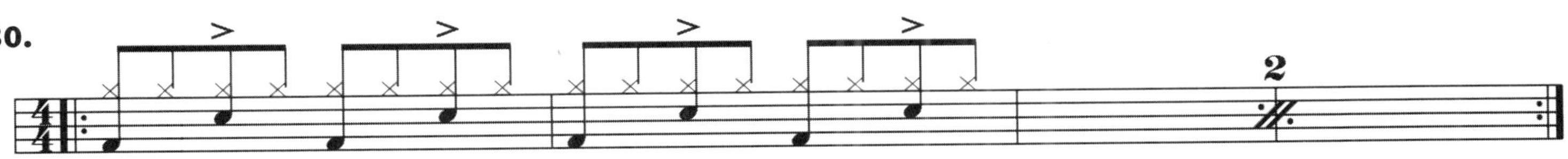

131.

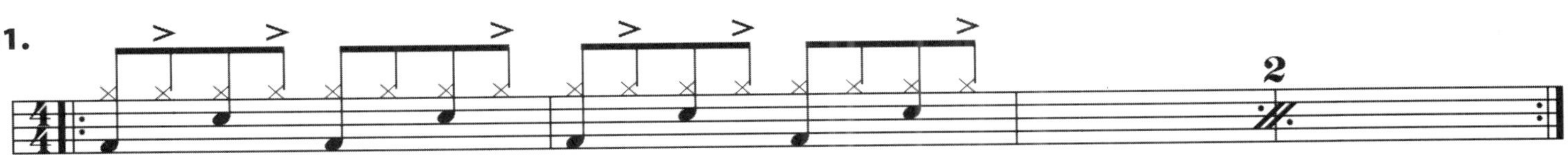

132.

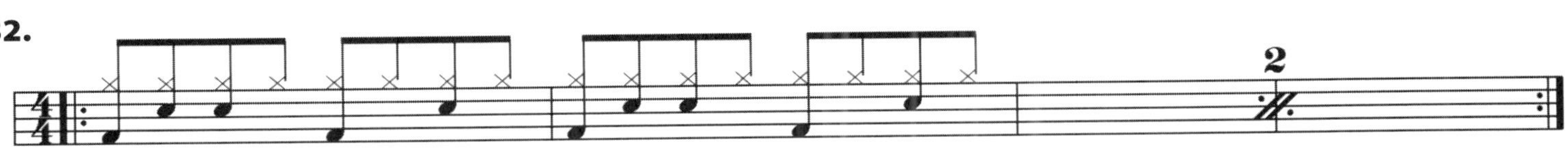

133.

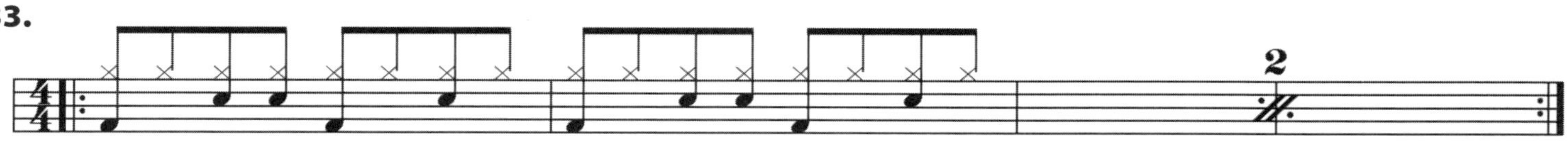

134.

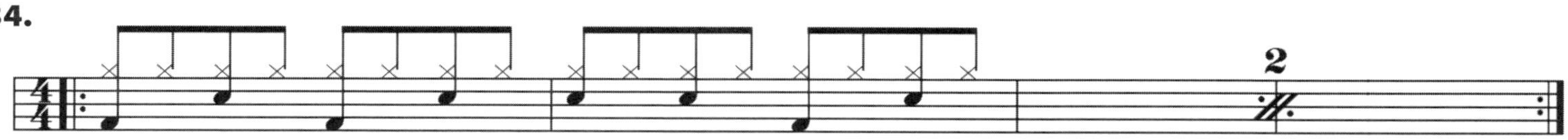

135.

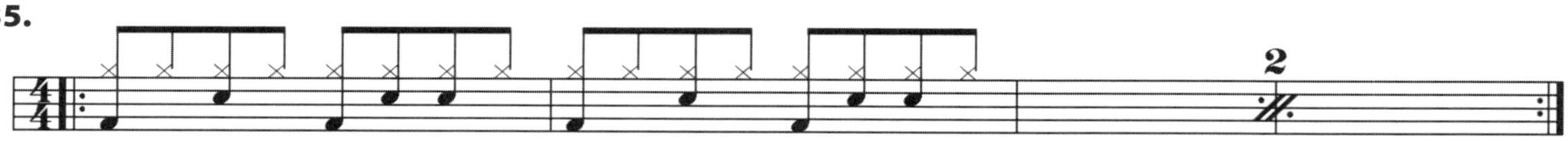

136.

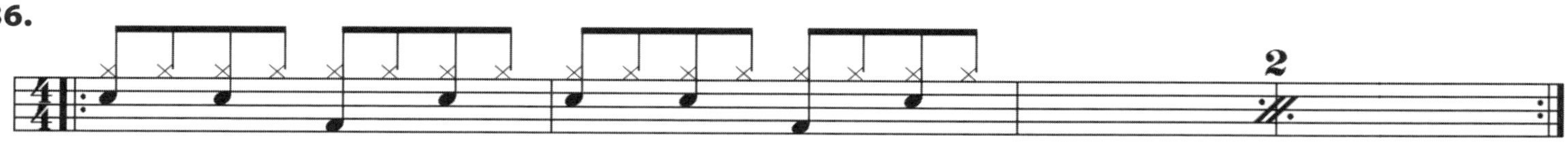

138.

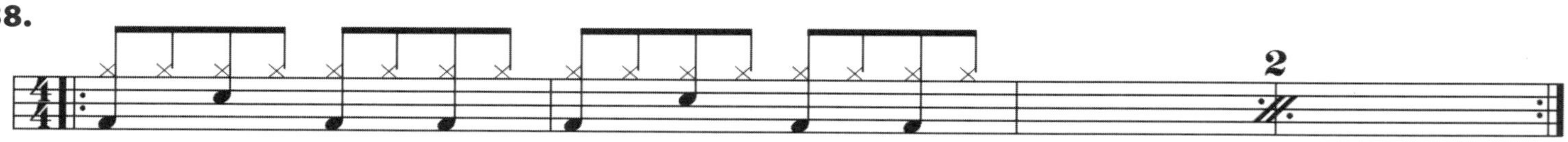

139.

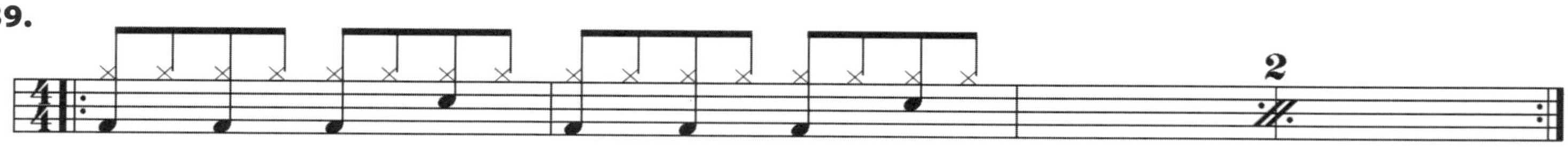

140.

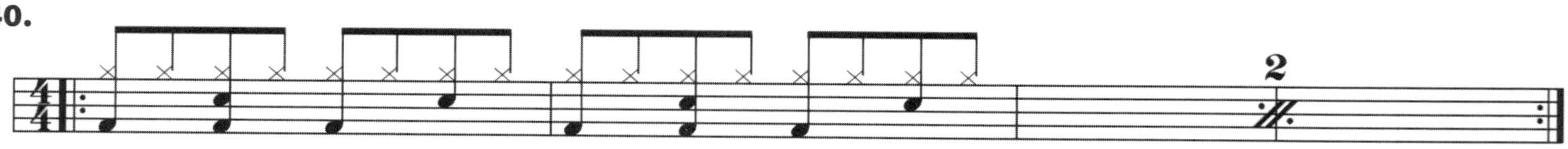

141.

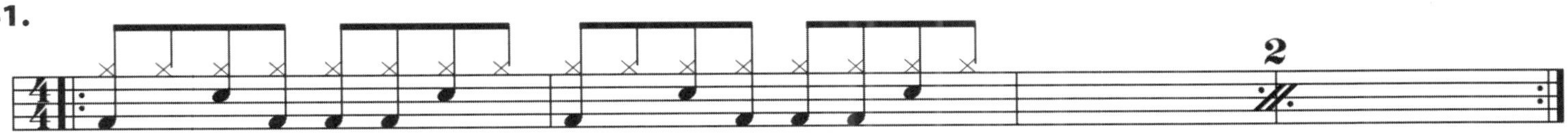

142.

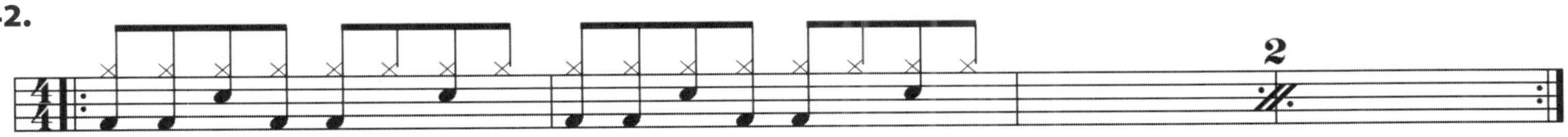

143.

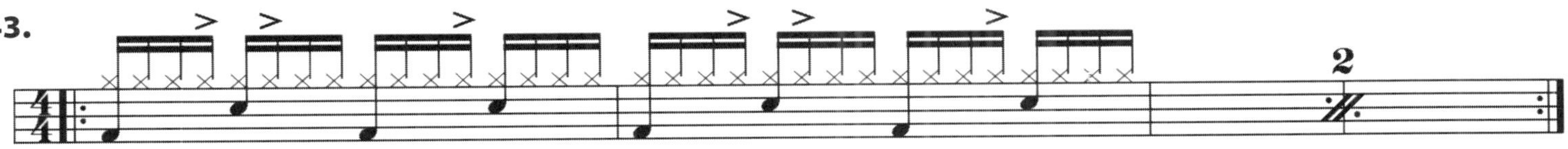

144.

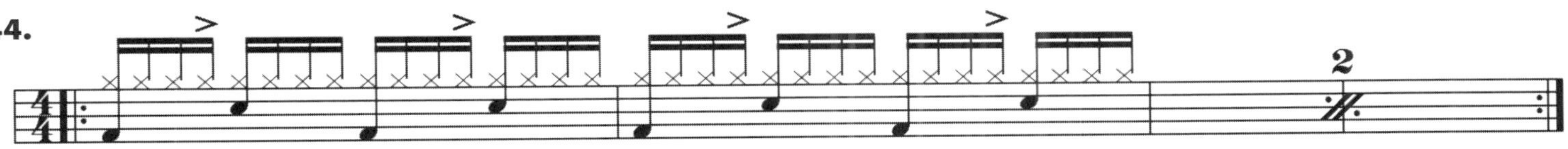

145.

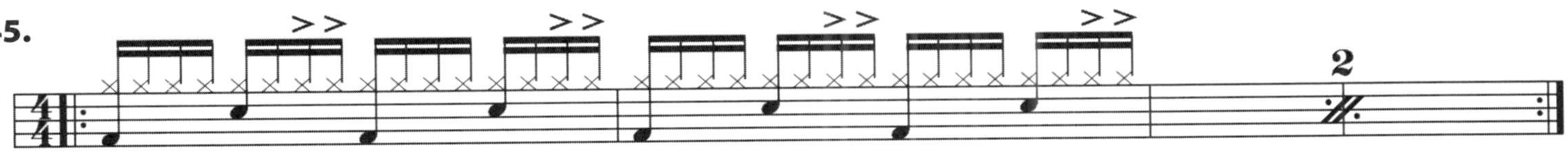

146.

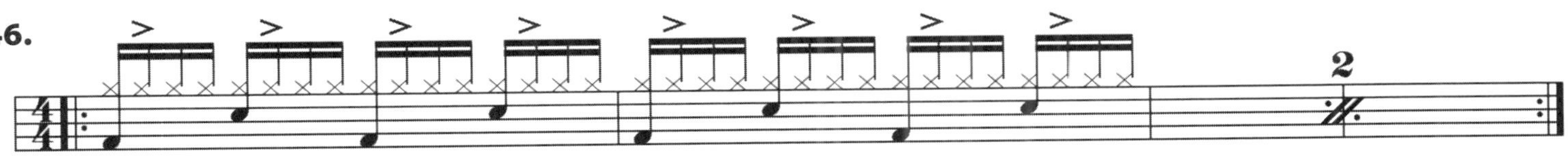

147.

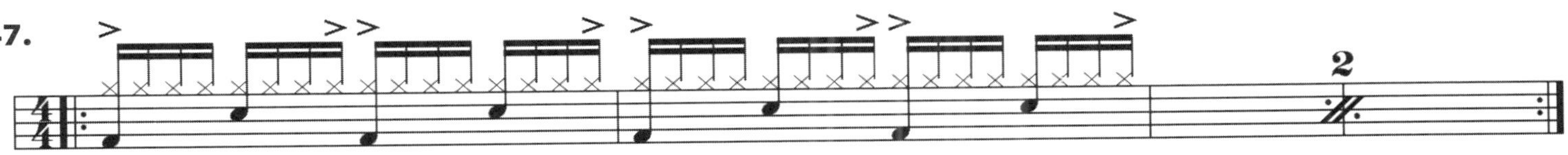

148.

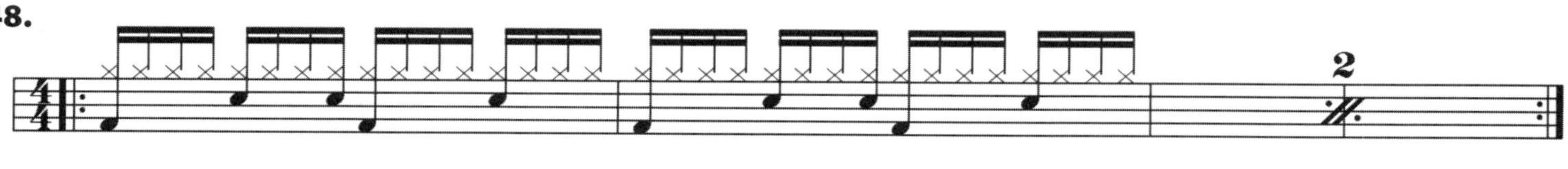

149.

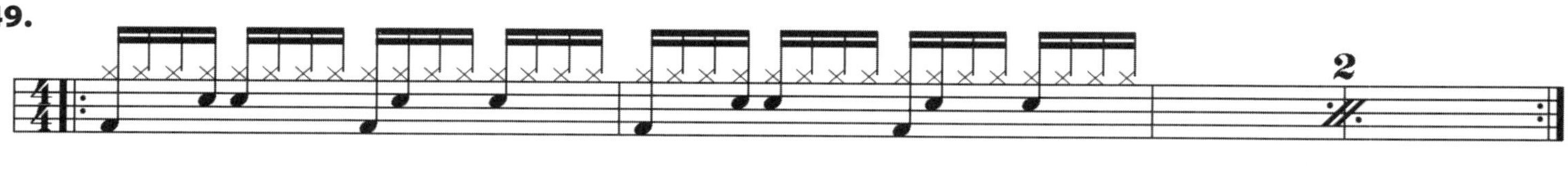

150.

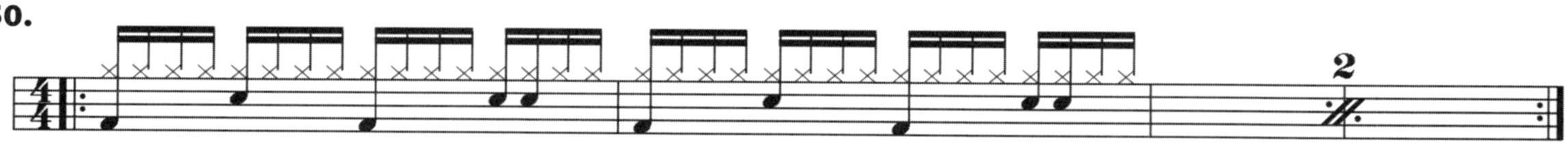

151.

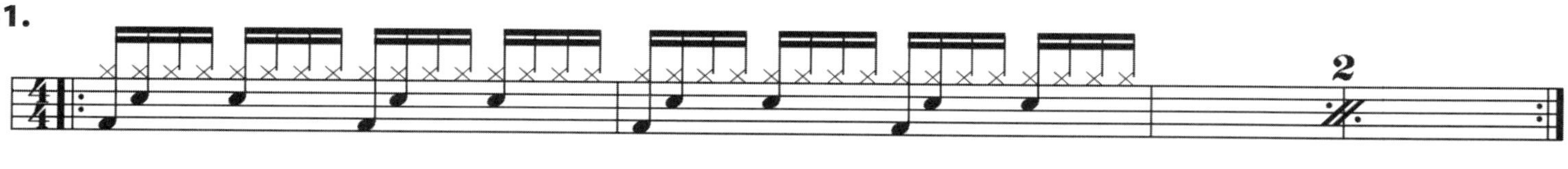

152.

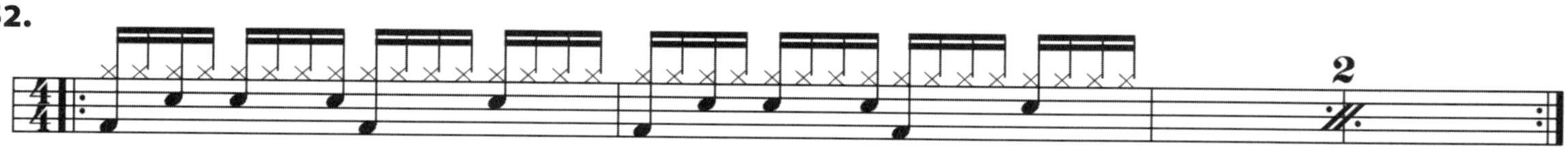

153.

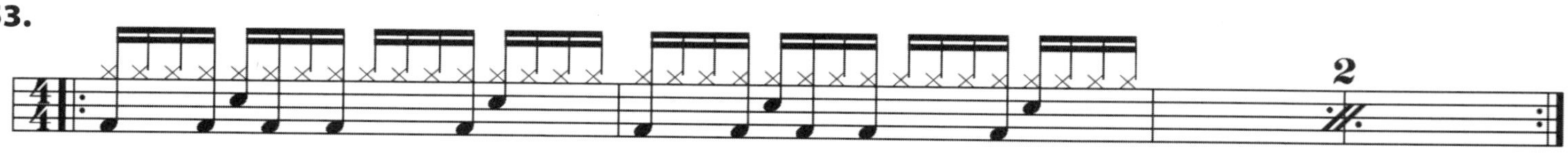

154.

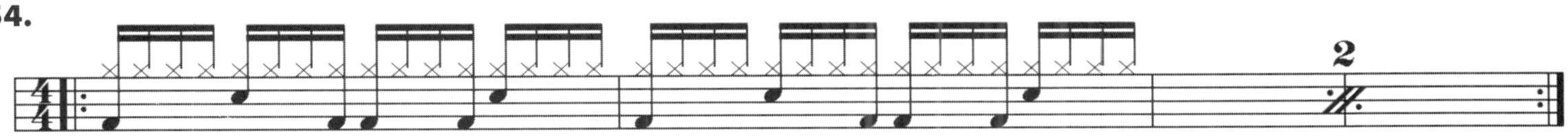

155.

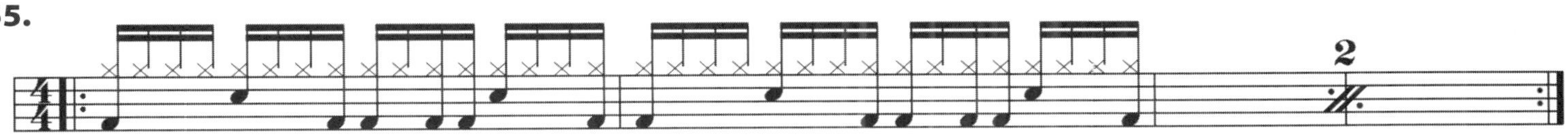

156.

157.

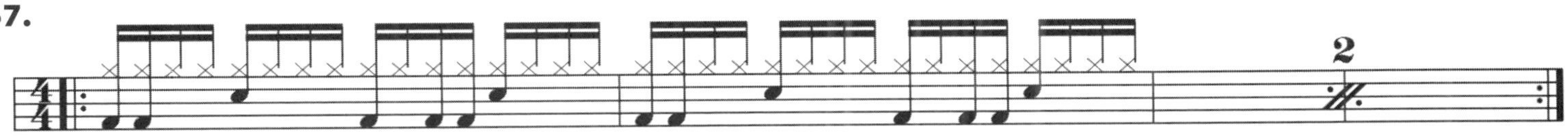

Crazy Combinations with Accents and Triplets

Here are some interesting combinations I play using different rhythms fused together.

158.

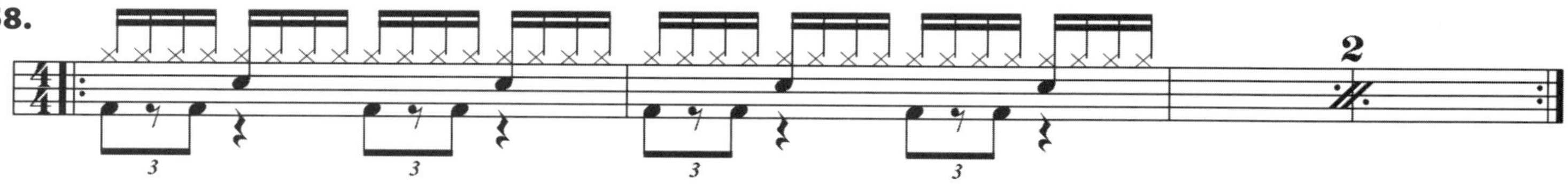

159.

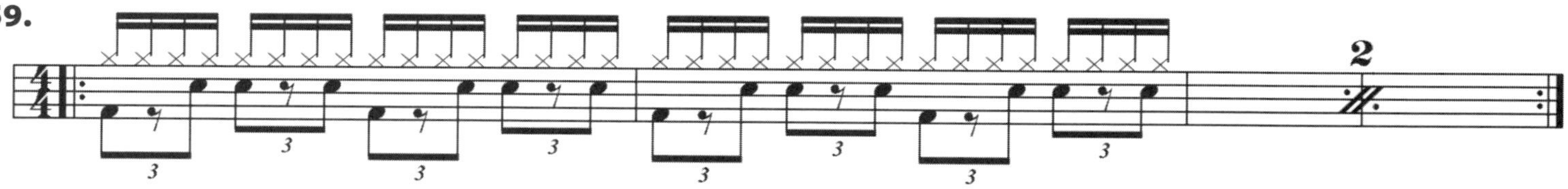

160.

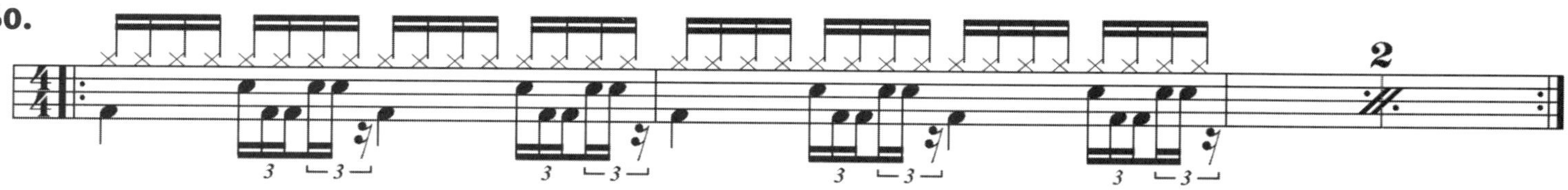

161.

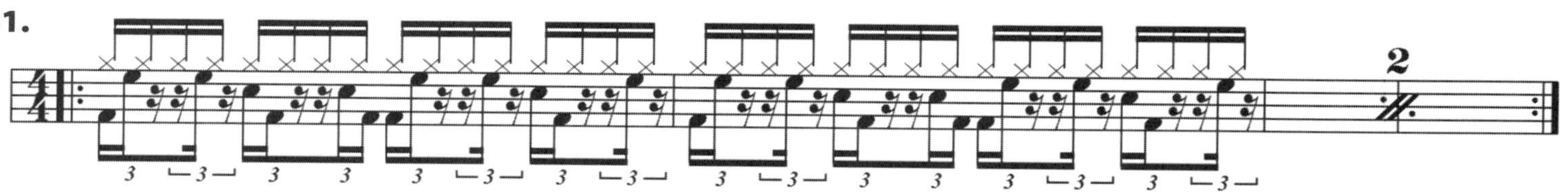

162.

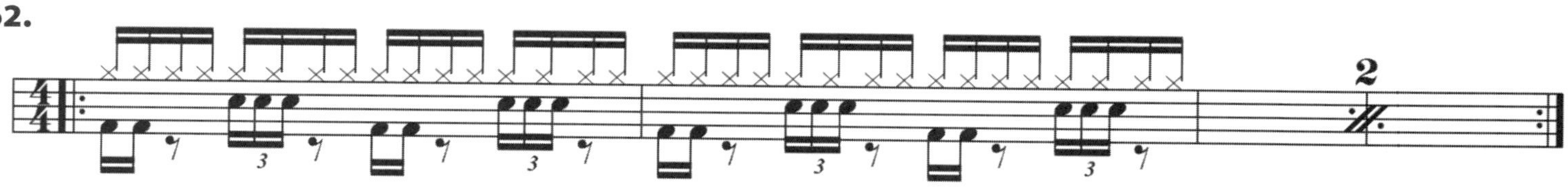

PERFORMANCE

Hand to Hand

As the name says, these patterns have hand-to-hand sticking, but they are not all on one sound source. This could also be referred to as a "linear" approach, with one sound source being played at a time.

163.

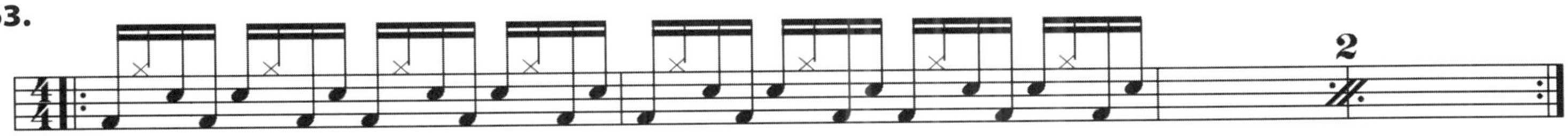

164.

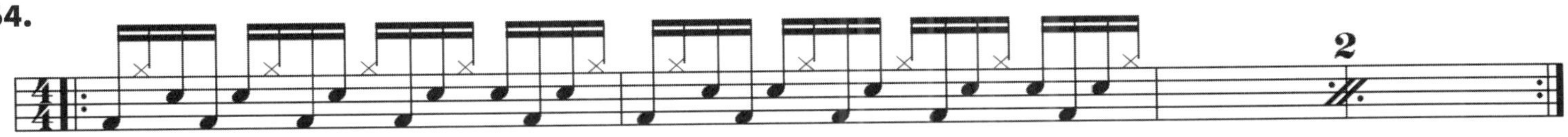

165.

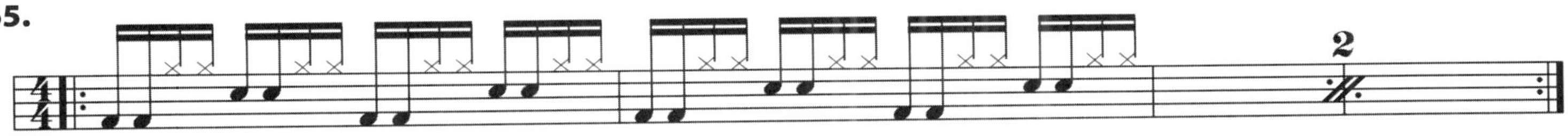

166.

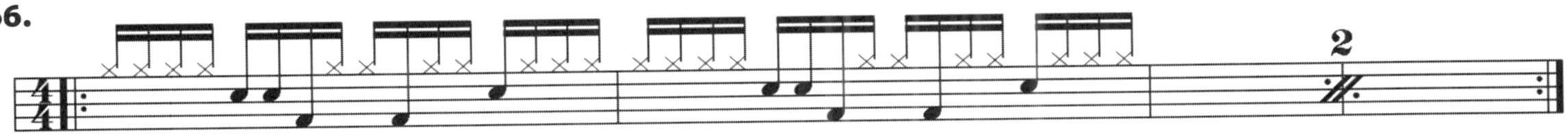

167.

PERFORMANCE

Study #19

Song Form (AABC)

Understanding how to play songs is crucial. In the studio or live, understanding how songs work will help your performance. We'll work with a standard song that has an intro and has different sections; let's say an "A" section, a "B" section, and a "C" section.

The "A" section will be like a verse.

"B" will be like a bridge.

The "C" will be like a kind of outro.

Since "A" is repeated, this type of song form would be referred to as AABC.

If you look at the chart, the beat changes from section to section. When transitioning from one section to the next, it's important to avoid speeding up or slowing down. The way to achieve this is to feel the subdivisions of what you're playing (as opposed to trying to count).

168.

PERFORMANCE

Study #20

The Power of the Loop

I love loops because whenever I play a loop, both I and the listener know or can predict what's about to happen next. When this happens, no one's thinking about the beat anymore. They're only looking forward to expecting what's going to happen and reacting to it before it even happens. And that kind of energy and concept is amazing. But that only happens when you're repeating the same thing over and over, without changing.

If you start playing a loop and it seems like the gel between you and the band (or the band and listeners) hasn't happened yet, keep doing it. About the third or fourth time, they'll get what you're doing.

The examples below aren't difficult per se, but they are great for practicing and understanding the power of the loop.

169.

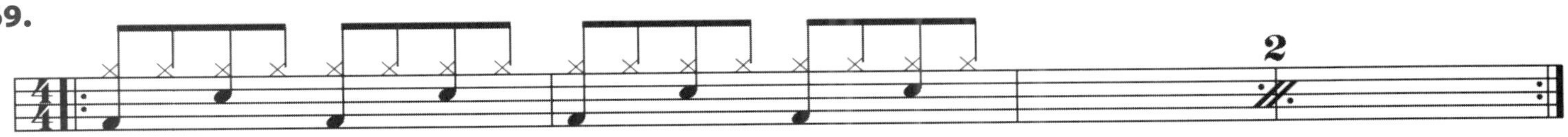

170.

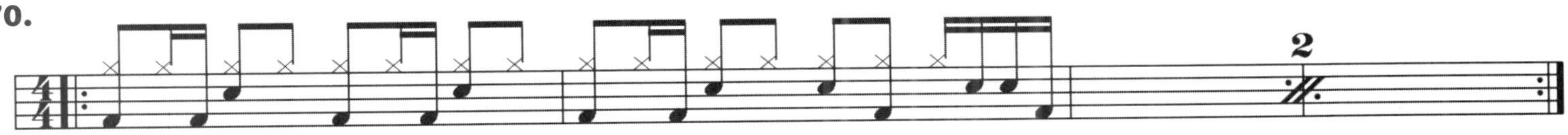

171.

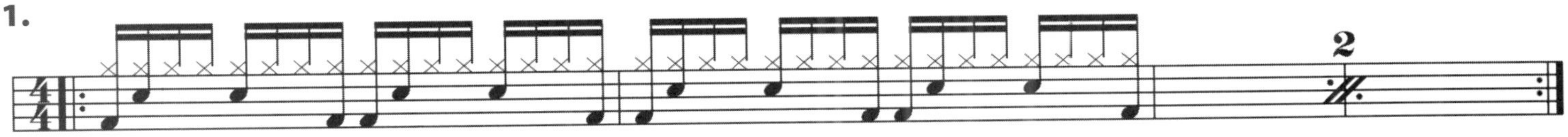

172.

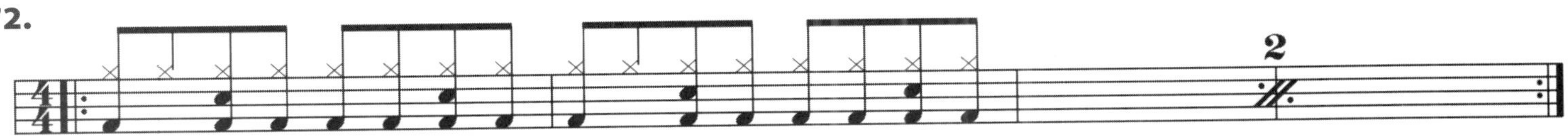

173.

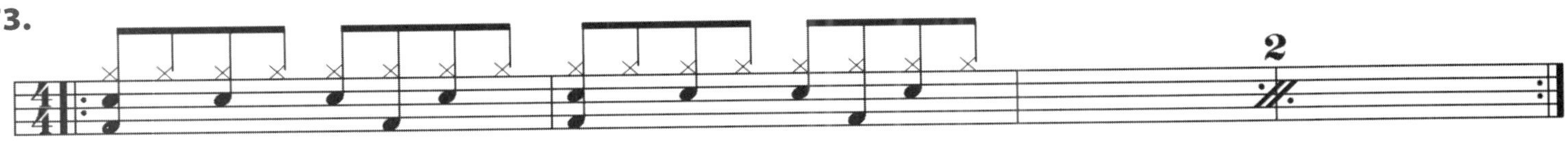

174.

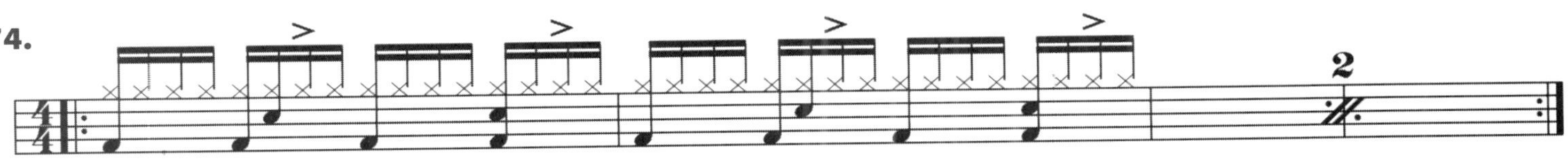

Study #21

Live vs. Studio

When it comes to playing live vs. in the studio, some things are different and some things are similar. I've noticed that in the studio, the attention to detail goes up a lot because it's more about capturing the nuances of the recording that's going to happen. In the studio, everything matters: the sound of the drums, the way you hit the drums and the cymbals, the way you understand how to play the song and the parts, etc. It's also important, if you're in the studio, to be able to translate whatever the song requires without overplaying or underplaying. Studio playing requires discipline.

Live, it's a little more loose. You have more freedom to be expressive. You still have to pay attention to detail and still have to play the right parts and sounds, but, now, the focus is different. It's about the performance.

Going from live to the studio, you will be dealing with different rooms and acoustical environments. You might need a different approach to playing in those different rooms. In the studio, it's a little more controlled. Normally, a studio is set to handle a controlled kind of environment for recording. But live, it can be totally different. Sometimes, you're outside. Sometimes you get a bad engineer. You need to be prepared for anything!

When I'm playing in the studio, I'm focused on the parts, tuning, and how to document the best performance possible. Live, I'm doing the same thing, but I'm also trying to convey a feeling to the bandstand and to the people in the audience.

The way you hit your drums and cymbals might change in the studio. For instance, when I'm playing in the studio, I try not to crash too abrasively. Even if I'm trying to get a lot of sound out of the cymbal, I try not to hit too hard.

IMPROVISATION

Improvisation can be a little intimidating to some players. Some players welcome it, and others get a little uncomfortable with it. I'll share some info and ideas that can help ease the process of practicing improvisation.

"Improvisation" can be a bad word in many genres, especially pertaining to beats. Some people think of improvising as a drummer playing too many fast notes, being selfish, or getting in the way. But this doesn't have to be the case. Understanding improvisation gives a drummer their own distinct personality and level of freedom like no other concept—especially when playing a beat.

"The key to improvising appropriately is how well you understand the language." The more information you gather, learn, and practice executing, the better you will become in improvising. Record yourself and write down your ideas!

On the video, I give you a chance to improvise with me by trading beats. I explain and demonstrate a beat, then you can play with me. I play four measures of groove, then lay out and provide space for you to improvise your own "answer" to what I have played. Have fun!

Study #22

Improv Exercises

These are rhythmic motifs for you to use to build improvisational ideas. I demonstrate some ideas with ex. 176 on the video.

175.

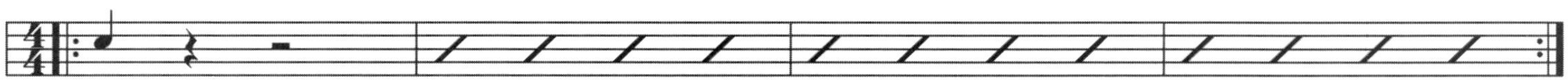

176.

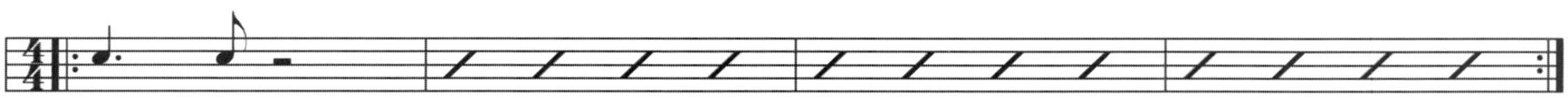

177.

178.

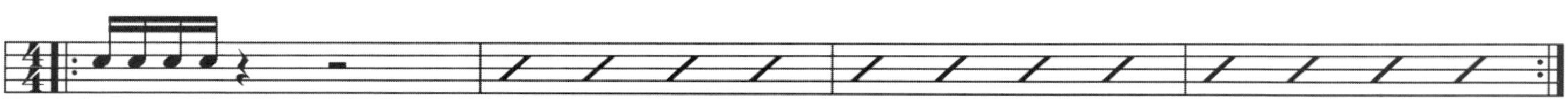

179.

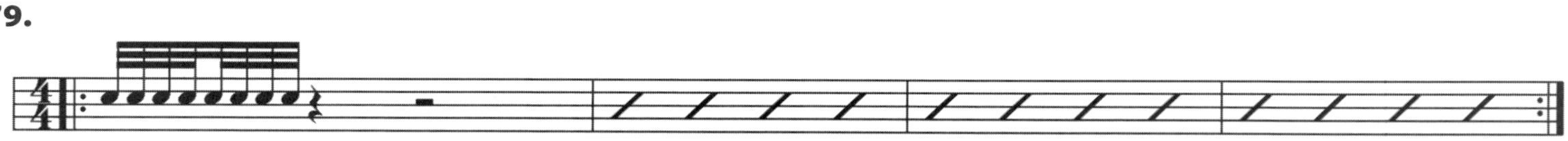

180.

181.

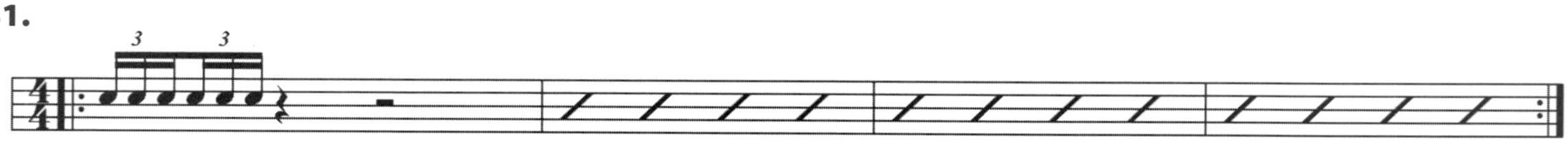

IMPROVISATION

182.

183.

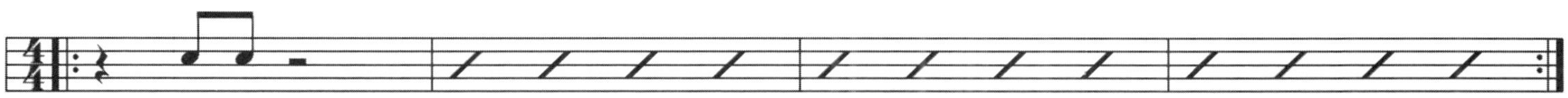

184.

185.

Improvise

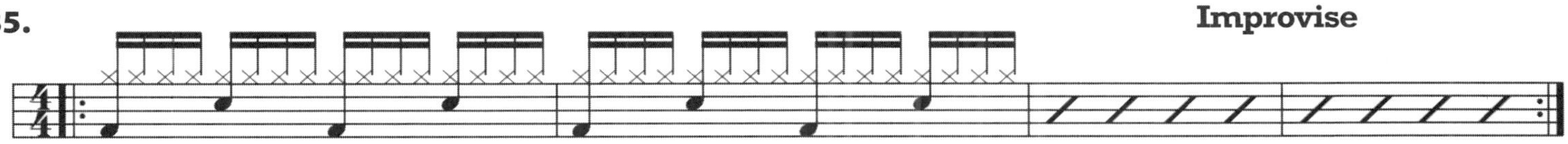

186.

Improvise

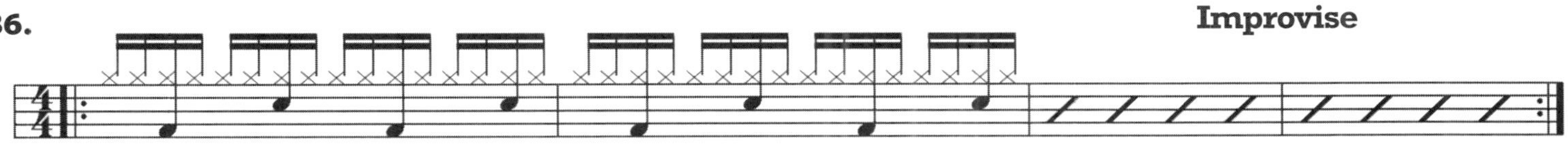

187.

Improvise

188.

Improvise

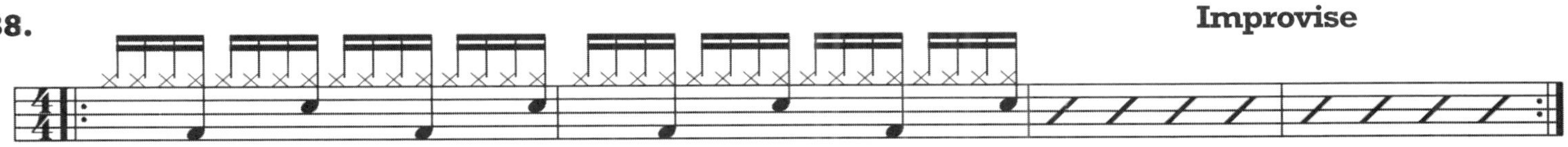

189.

Improvise

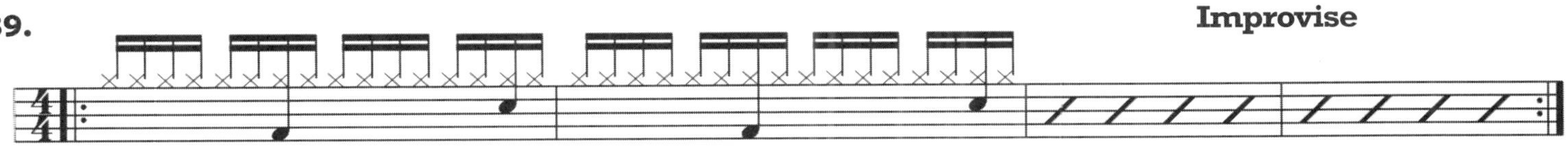

IMPROVISATION

Study #23

Discover Your Voice

When you improvise with motifs enough, you will hear and further develop your voice. In these examples, I have provided two bars of an idea, then you improvise two bars to complete the phrase. Improvise your own way. You can play the same thing, a contrast, or anything you want. Improvise however you hear it and be comfortable in what you hear. Remember: your thoughts and ideas are good! Be confident in that.

190.

191.

192.

193.

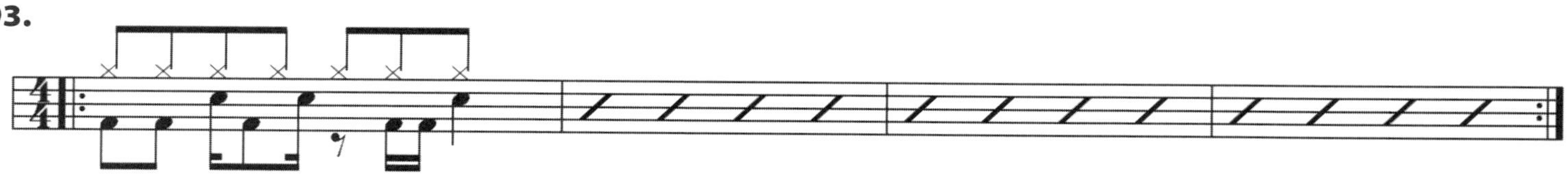

194.

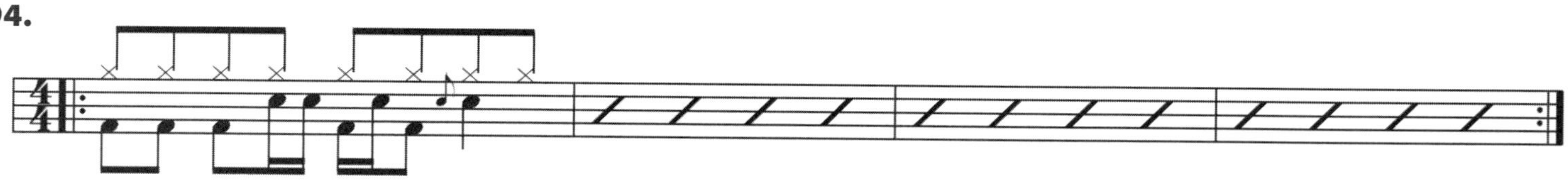

Study #24

Defining Your Voice

Here are some more example to hopefully encourage your creativity. In these examples, the first two bars represent a **cadence**, or thematic rhythm. I then play a two bar groove to with the cadence. Keep in mind the two-bar groove doesn't necessarily have to match the cadence rhythm exactly.

195.

196.

197.

198.

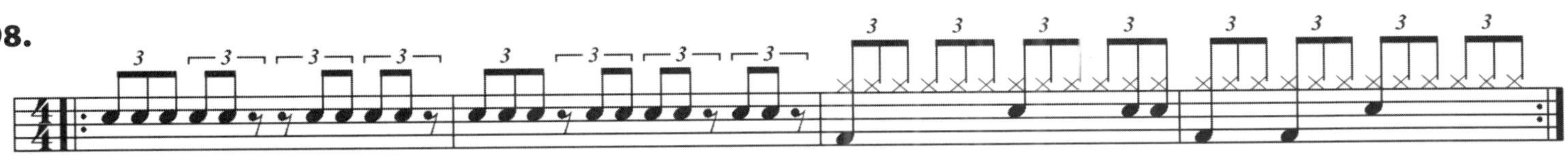

199.

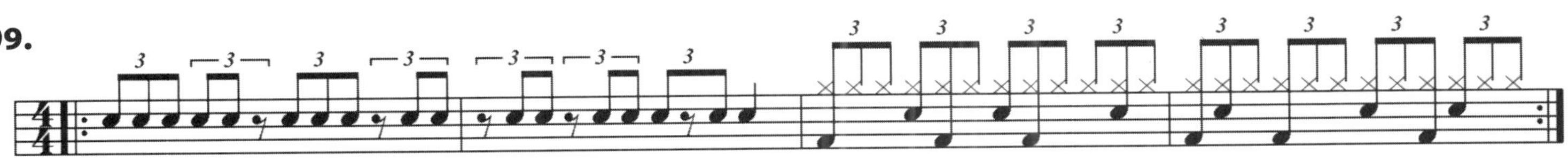

200.

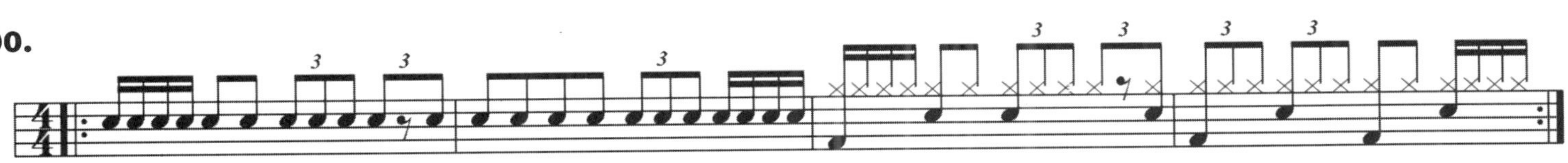

IMPROVISATION

Study #25

Inspiration

These are some different ideas for you to expand on as you improvise.

201.

202.

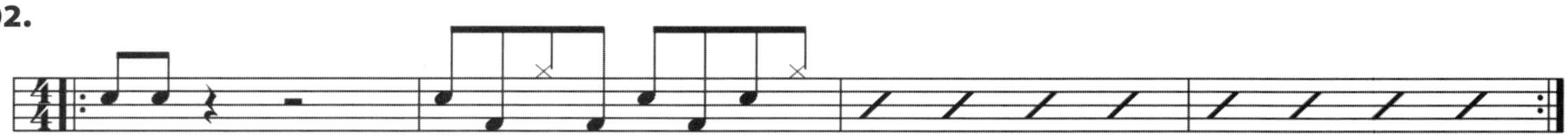

203.

204.

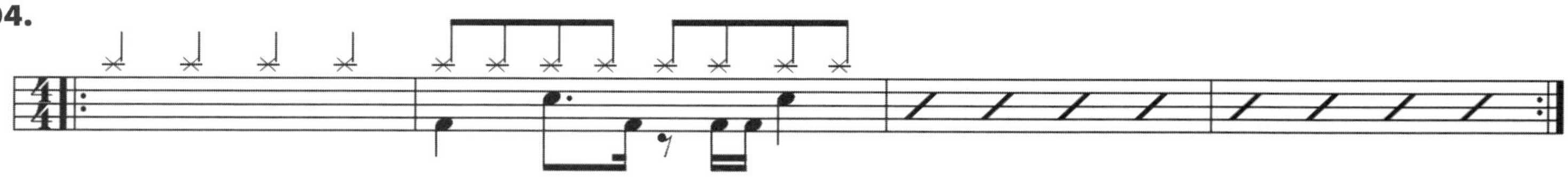

205.

Study #26

Communication: Tension & Release

Tension and release is an important concept in music. When piano players play, certain chord progressions create tension and then, in contrast to the tension that's created, there are certain chord progressions, or chords, that provide release. This same concept happens rhythmically, and when this is understood, you're able to be more expressive and interact on a higher level with the people that you're playing with.

In the video, I use example 210 to play four different forms of tension and release in a little solo.

Drummers create tension and release in the following ways:

Fills

Every time a drummer does a fill, it creates tension because there is a need to resolve the fill back to the beat. If I started playing a fill, and just kept playing the fill over and over again, after a while, you're going to want to hear the beat again. This affects songs heavily; some drummers that don't understand this concept create tension and don't create the proper release, or they create tension where there needs to be resolution, because they don't understand what's happening. They may do fills in the wrong place. They may play beats in places where they should do fills, or they may play with no dynamics.

Dynamics

Another way to cause tension and to release is through dynamics. Many drummers seem to not to understand that when you play soft, it causes tension, because it creates a certain curiosity of what's about to happen. It's very suspenseful. Check out the video for a demonstration of this. Notice, when I hit the cymbal at the end of the demo, it was, like, "Oh, that's the end. That's where he was going with all of the suspense that he created in going soft and then getting louder. I was wondering what was going to happen." That's dynamics!

Space, partial playing or not playing at all creates great tension in which can make for a dramatic release.

Playing an Odd Number of Bars or an Odd Phrase

By playing an odd number of bars, you create tension. On the video I play an odd number of bars and then get back to an even number of bars so you can see this version of tension and release. You can see I was in 4 and then went to 3 and back to 4. You'll hear how going to 3 created tension, and going back to 4 released it.

Sonically

Your choice of sounds can create this effect as well—going from an open hi-hat sound to a closed hi-hat sound or playing a deep snare versus a high-pitched snare. Exploring going between various sounds can also help expand your vocabulary of how to cause tension and release.

IMPROVISATION

Tension 1

206.

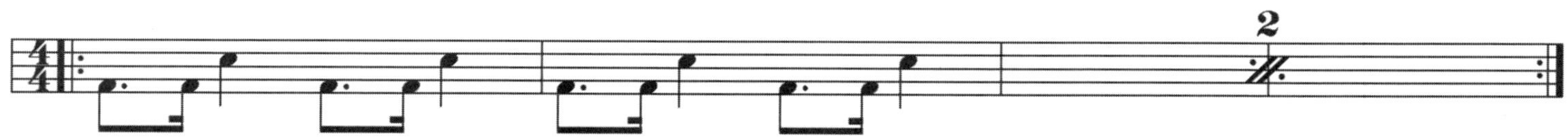

Tension 2

207.

Tension 3

208.

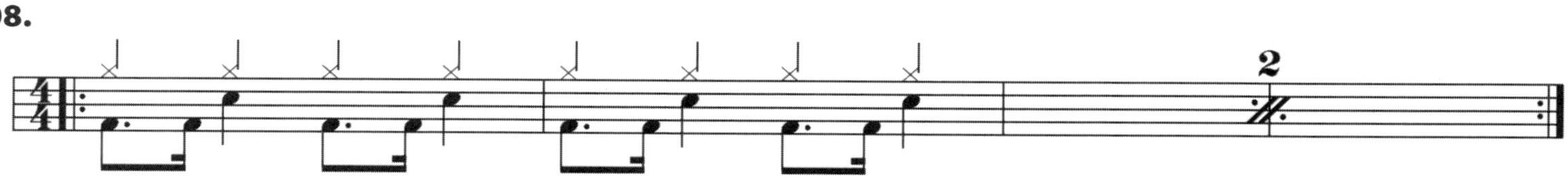

Release

209.

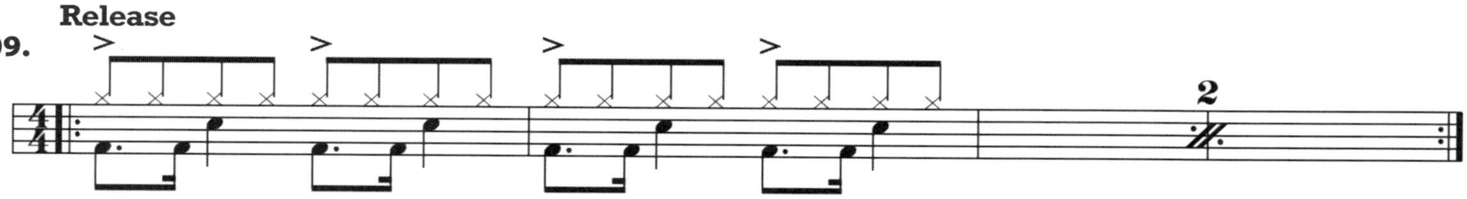

Dynamics

210.

Partial Playing

211.

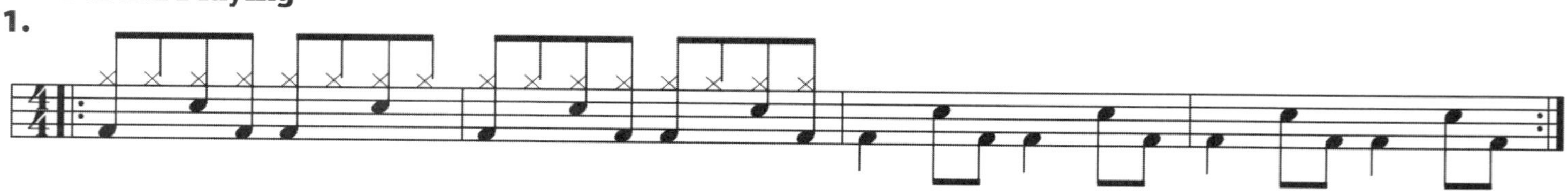

IMPROVISATION

Study #27

Comping

Comping is a combination of musical improvisation and dialogue. It is supporting a melody, rhythm, or feeling in a conversational type of way. Here some comping concepts for each rhythmic theme.

Rhythmic Melody

212.

Rhythmic Melody

213.

Rhythmic Melody

214.

Rhythmic Melody

215.

CHOP CLASS

I love all the aspects of drumming, but this is a special one because it is a very personal expression and it's fun. Facility on the drum set can be expressed in a solo or band setting in so many different ways. This part focuses on the band setting. A lot of drummers think one-dimensionally when approaching chops in beats, but what I would like to do is provide a few more dimensions of explorations. The great part is when you discover your own ways and concepts of communicating this way, you'll have a lot more depth to what you play.

> "A picture can say a thousand words, but a few words can paint a whole picture."

Often, drummers think of chops as just playing a lot of different kinds of fills. But, through the years, I've discovered that there's more to it than that. I realized this after playing in different kinds of situations. I would play a fill, only to find out that the fill didn't work musically with the band that I was playing with. So this caused me to take a fresh at look at chops. A chop doesn't have to be a fill.

With this concept you can also take different nuances and apply them to whatever it is that you do. So, if you're a rock drummer, you'll maybe play some jazz language. Or, if you play gospel, and that's your main thing, and you try some rock-style fills, understanding the nuances of the chops in those different genres will help you do that.

On the video I explain and demonstrate some basic stylistic chop ideas, including hip-hop, jazz, rock and gospel chops.

CHOP CLASS

Study #28

Chop Language

Hip Hop Chops

216.

217.

Patterns

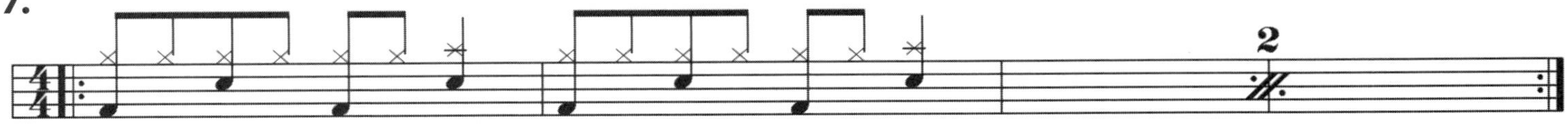

218.

Sonics

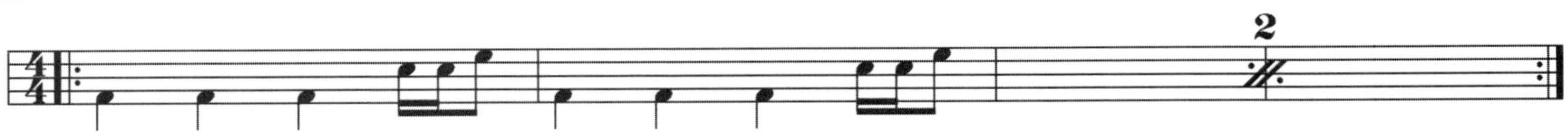

219.

Feel

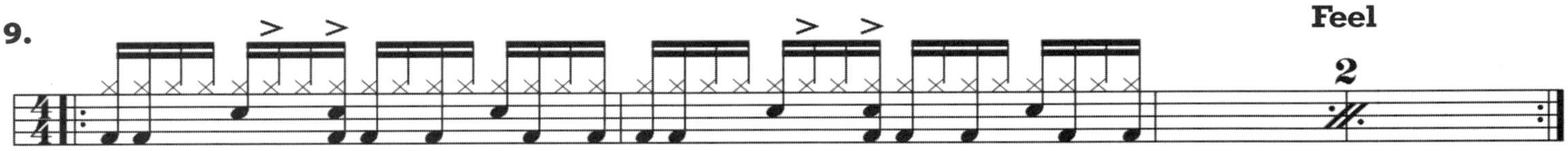

Swing Chops

220.

221.

Lyrical

222.

Swing Chops cont'd

223. **Witty**

224. **Finesse**

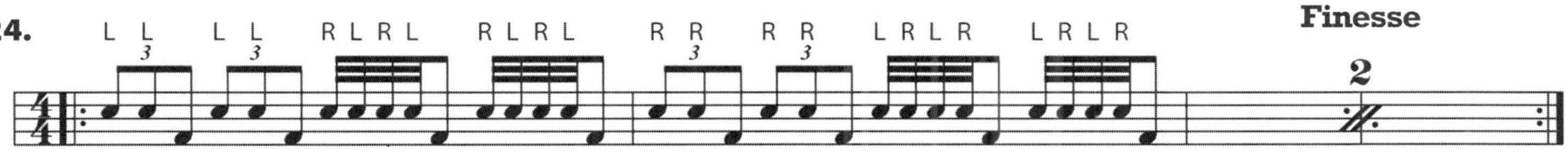

Rock Chops

225.

226. **Power**

227. **Anthem**

228. **Open**

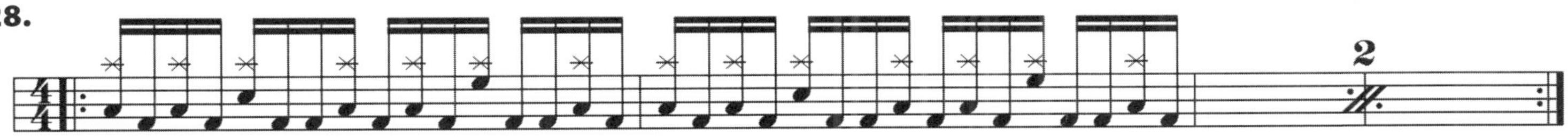

229.

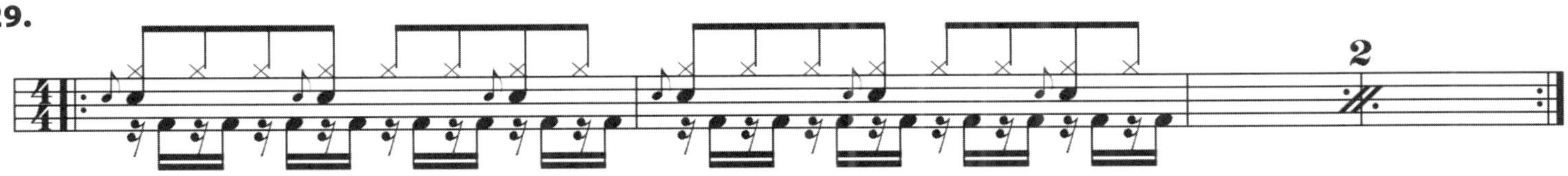

Gospel Chops

230.

Emotional

231.

Complex

232.

233.

Funky

234.

CHOP CLASS

Study #29

Independence

Example 236 is a 4-way independence challenge. The feet are playing in 3/4 (bass drum on 1, hi-hat on 2 and 3). The ride is playing the 4/4 swing beat, and the snare is playing a rhythm in 5/8. See the video for a demonstration of this and several other concepts from this section. The key for doing this section accurately is for all the independence exercises to strongly groove.

Play hi-hat on 2 & 4.

235.

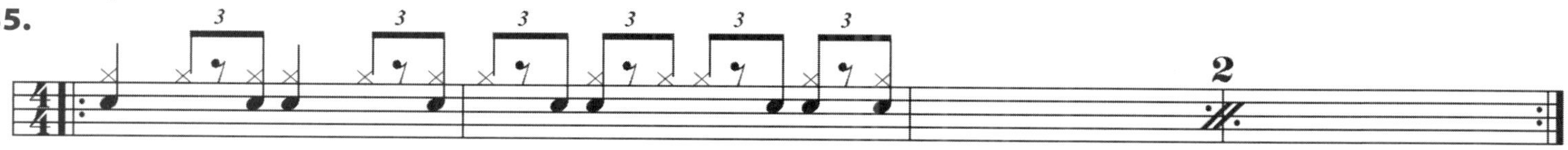

The co-ordination challenge. Start with the foot pattern, then add the ride, then the snare. You can do it!

236.

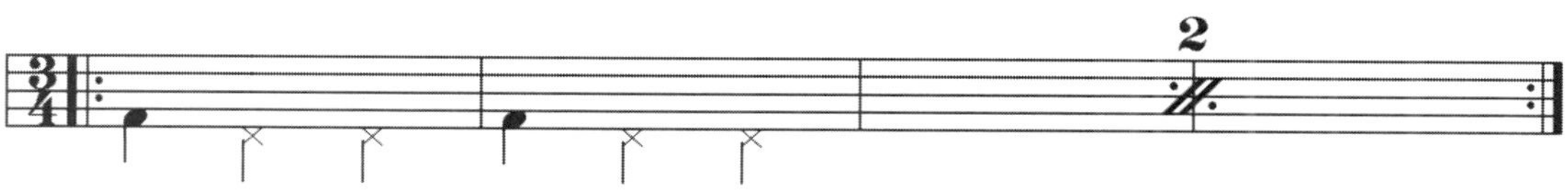

236 a.

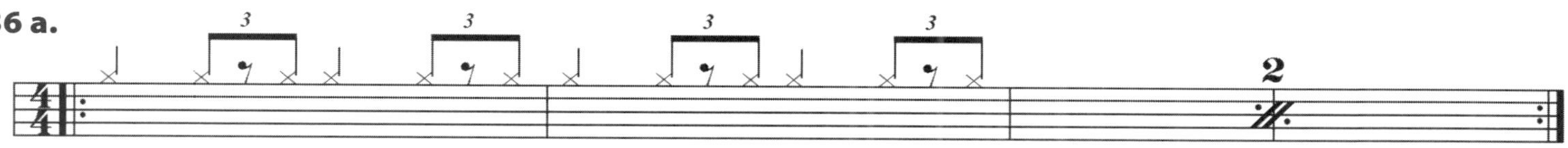

236 b.

237.

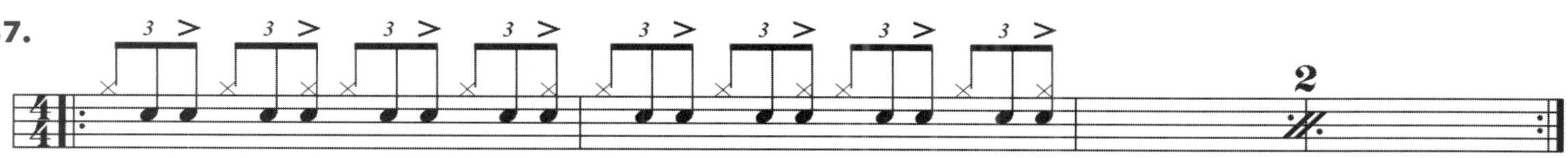

Now apply the hi-hat and bass drum patterns below to ex. 237.

237 a.

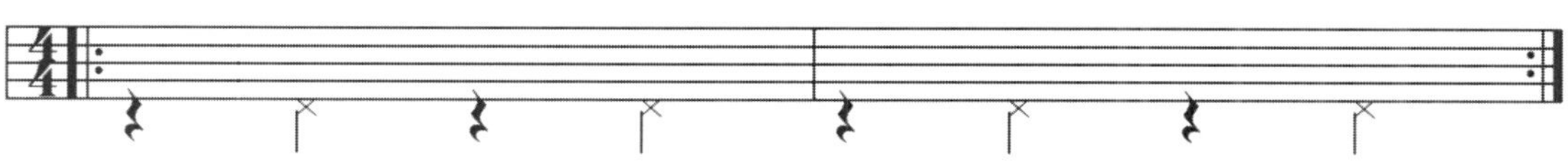

238.

Play these patterns with the ride playing the basic swing pattern while keeping the hi-hat on 2 & 4.

239.

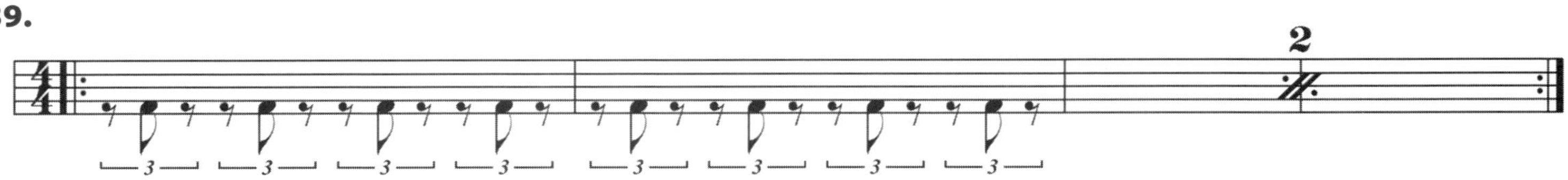

240.

241.

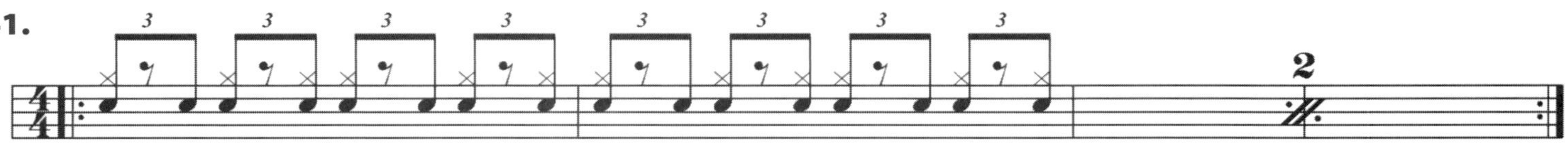

242.

243.

Here, try to make sure the bass drum is as quiet as possible using feathering techniques while keeping the hi-hat & ride strong.

244.

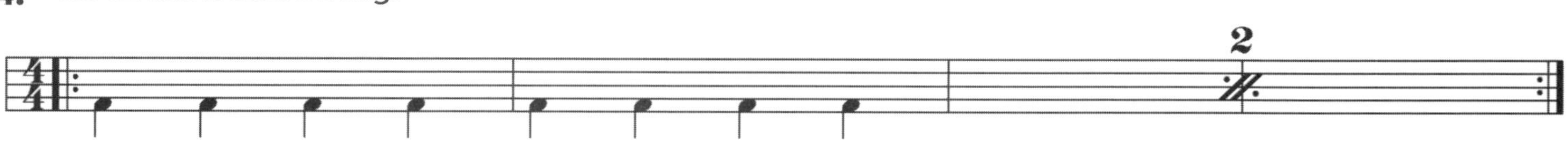

245.

CHOP CLASS

Being able to play notes together inside of a groove helps to strengthen your independence. Use a basic swing pattern with hi-hat on 2 & 4 to practice these.

246.

247.

248.

Let's try some straight-16th independence exercises. We'll play the hi-hat on 1 & 3 for ex. 249-250. Sometimes seemingly simple things can become complex ideas.

249 a.

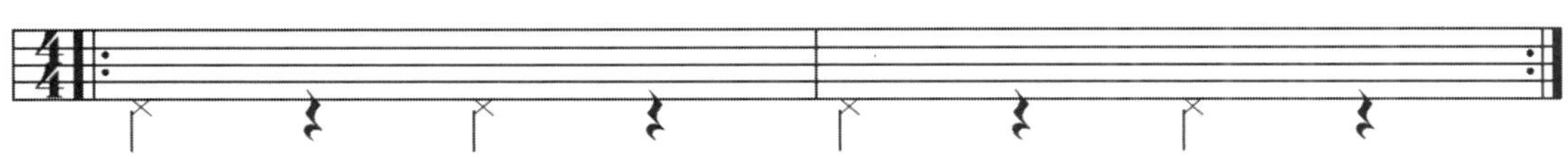

249.

250.

Let's change the hi-hat foot to play on the "and" of each beat for exercises 251 and 252.

251a.

251.

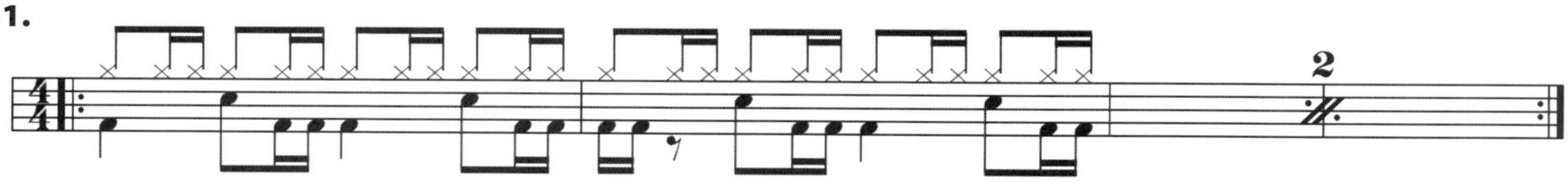

252.

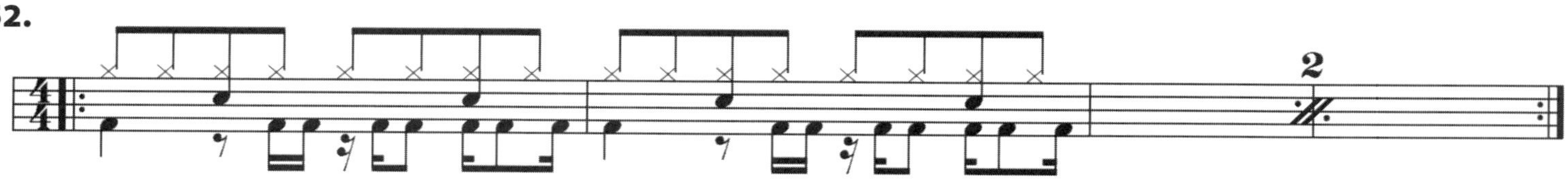

Here we will play the foot hi-hat pattern on fours while playing exercise 253. Remember, while trying to master this concept, it's OK to take chances and play other ideas while keeping fours with the hi-hat foot.

253a.

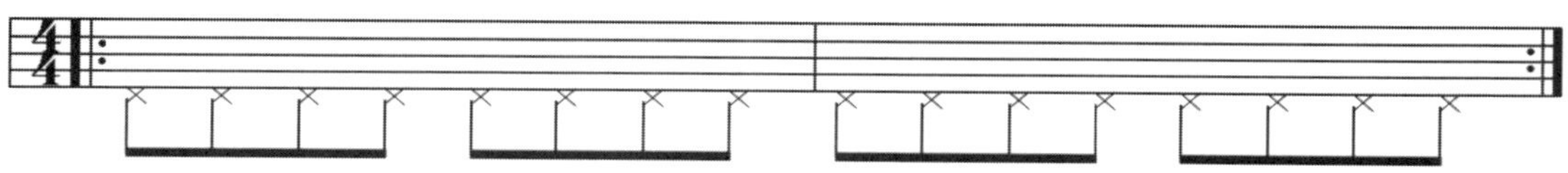

253.

CHOP CLASS

Study #30

Tension and Release

I liken this study to breathing. Inhaling air creates a tension to let the air out. Releasing the air satisfies the tension of inhaling. Chops work the same way. Even though we've talked about this briefly, exploring this concept even more will help add a lot of depth to your chops in any situation. There are a lot of ways to approach this, but here are a few exercises to explore.

T = Tension
R = Release

254.

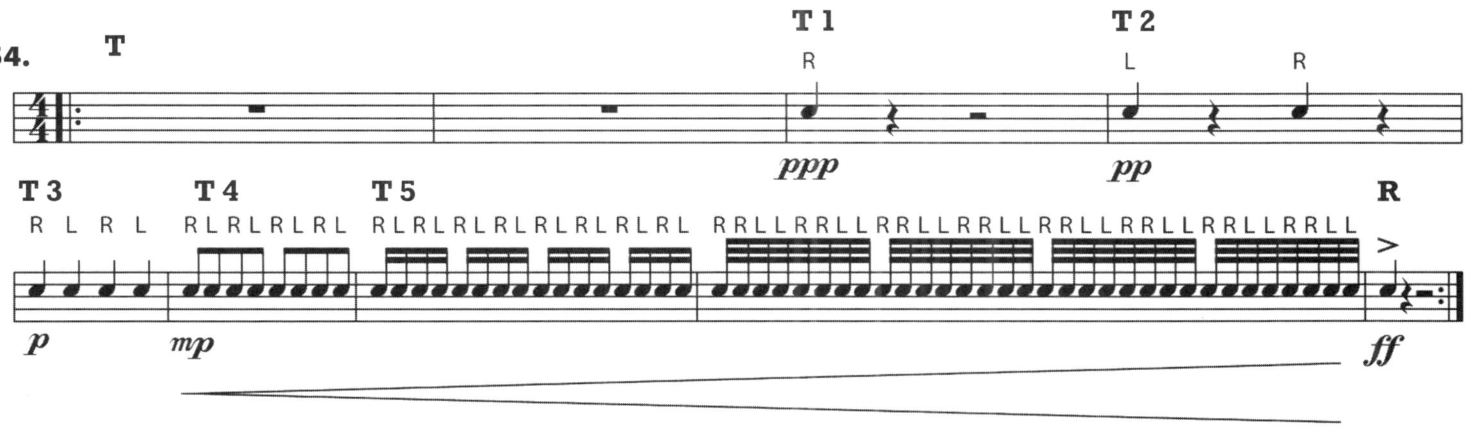

255.

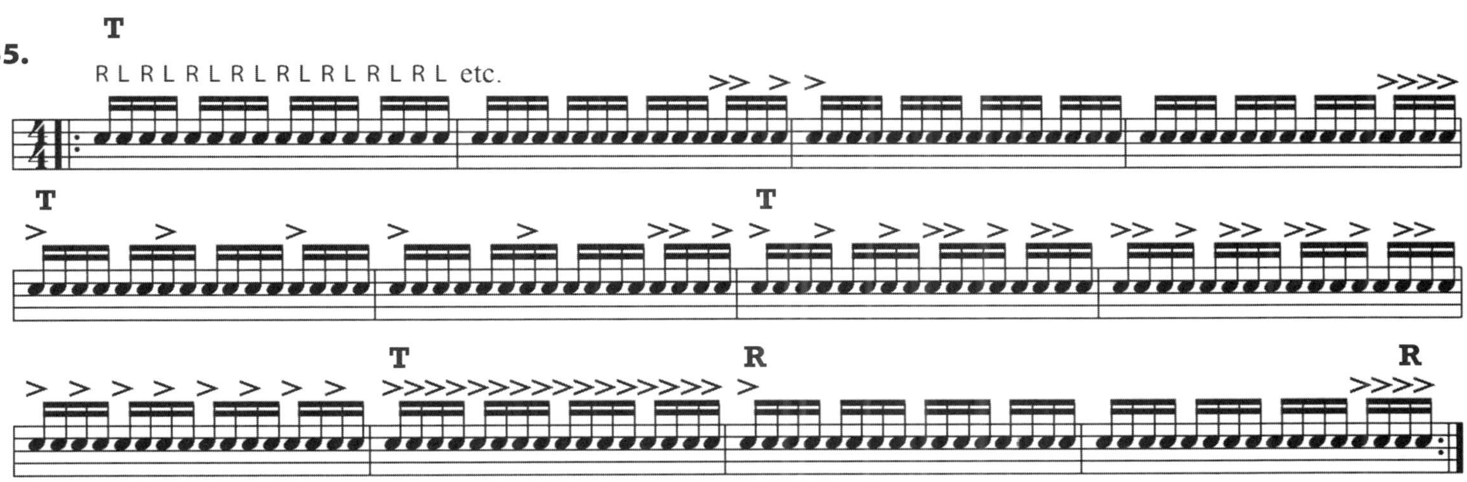

256.

257.

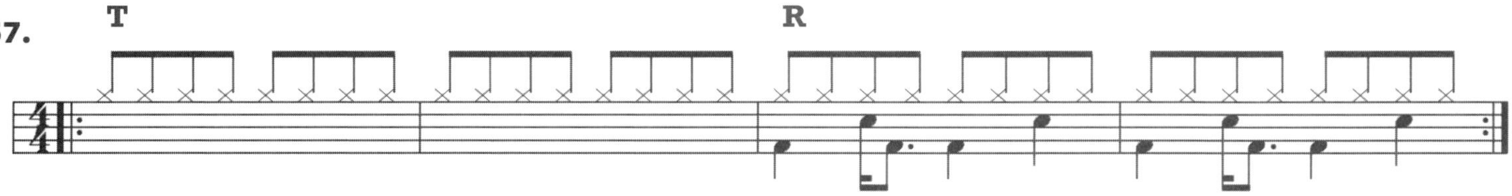

258.

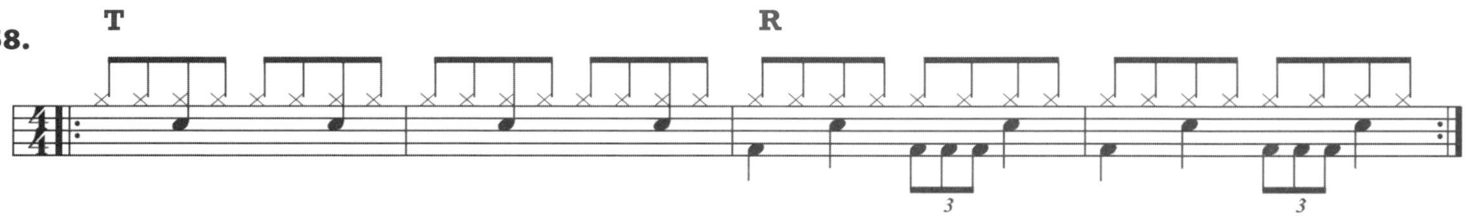

259.

CHOP CLASS

Study #31

Repetition, Call and Response

Another dimension to chops is repetition, taking a theme and repeating it over and over in different ways. I've discovered that the more something is repeated, the more I remember it, whether I want to or not. This comes in handy when you want someone to follow along with your ideas.

Then you have call and response. This communicative way of playing is very useful to add flow to your playing. Instead of trying to come up with rudiments or complex fills, being able to hear rhythm and communicate with it creates a dialogue that interesting to hear, and fun to play.

Here are some exercises to work on hearing both concepts.

Repetition

260.

261.

262.

263.

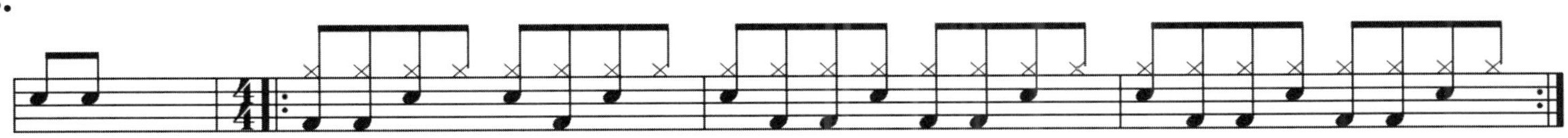

Call and Response Phrasing

C = Call **R** = Response

264.

265. C R

266. C R

267. C R

268. C R

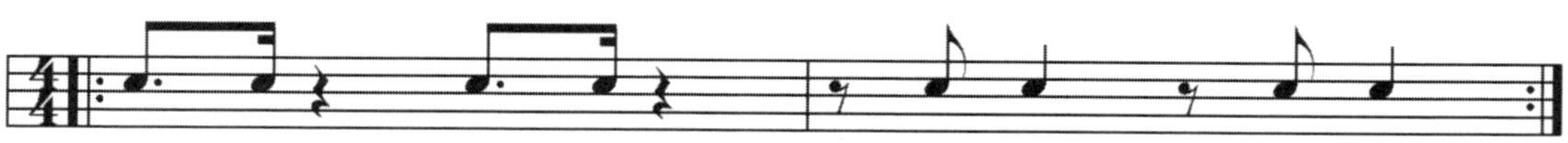

269. C R

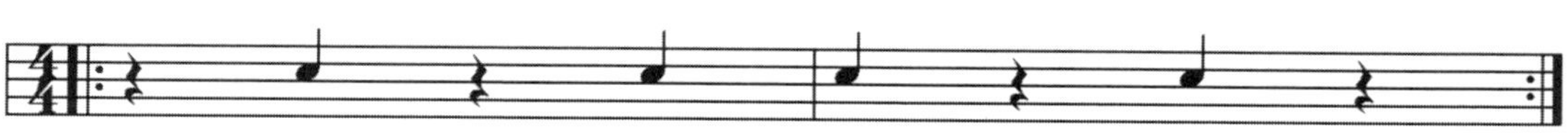

270. C R

271. C R

272. C R

273. C R

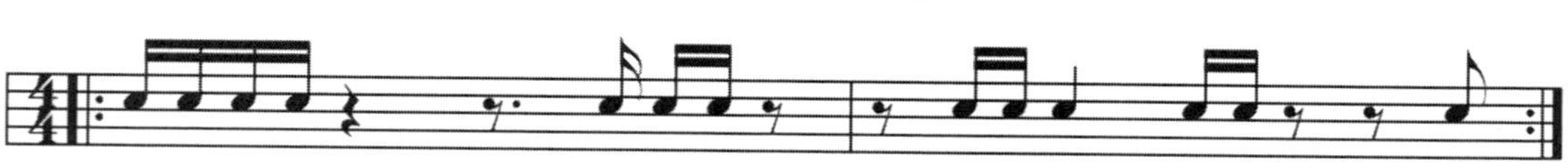

274. **C** **R**

275. **C** **R**

Now let's get more creative.

Here I have written the call, but you respond to it by writing in the rhythm or playing the phrase on a drum. The key to this is to practice hearing and playing rhythm in it's simplest form. Doing this will open your ears to a world of listening expression in conjunction with simple as well as very complex rhythms, providing unlimited possibilities in engaging the language of rhythm.

C = Call **U** = You respond

276. **C** **U**

277. **C** **U**

278. **C** **U**

279. **C** **U**

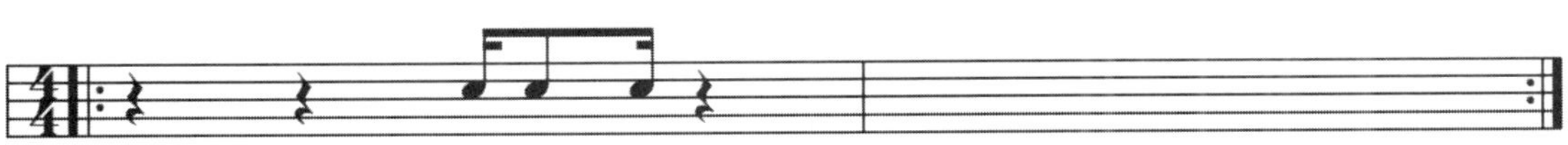

CHOP CLASS

280. C U

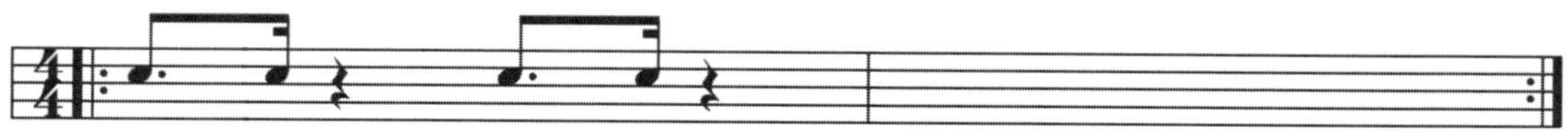

281. C U

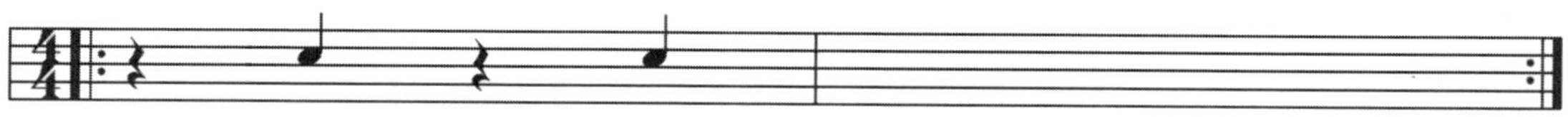

282. C U

283. C U

284. C U

285. C U

286. C U

287. C U

288. C U

289.
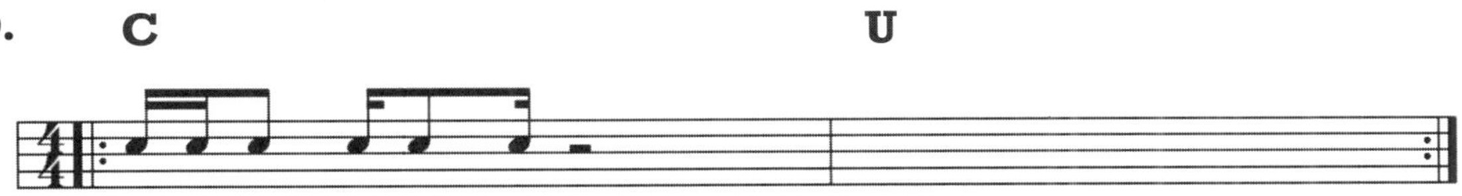

290.

291.

292.
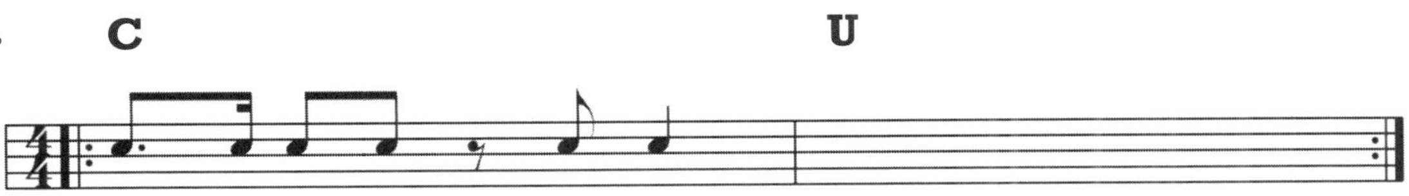

293.
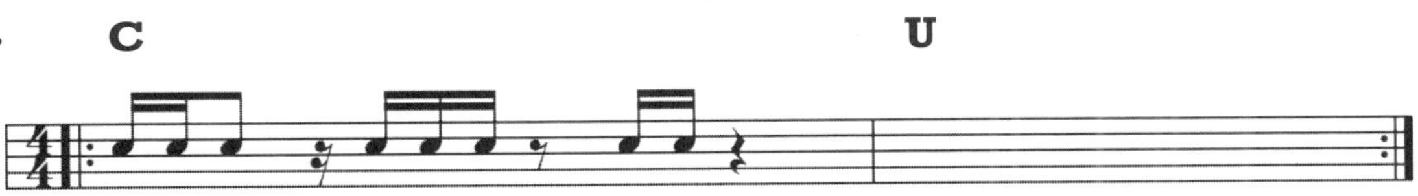

294.

295.

296.
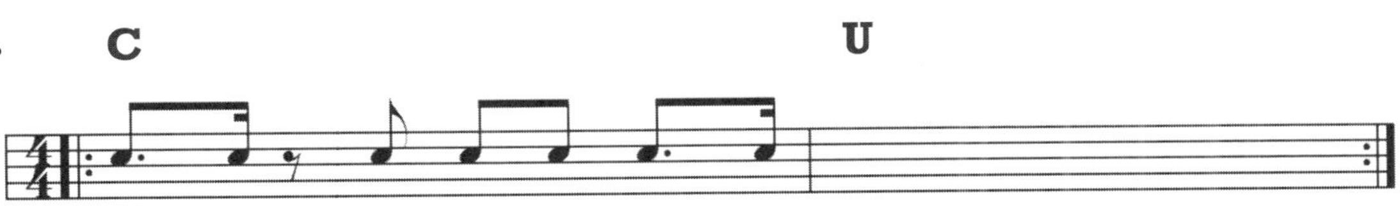

297.

CHOP CLASS

Study #32

Inversions

Playing things in a forward way is great, but flipping them backwards gives whatever that was played a unique sound and concept. Here we will explore some inversions to expand our rhythmic thinking.

298.

299.

300.

301.

302.

303.

304.

305.

306.

306a.

306b.

CHOP CLASS

Study #33

Punctuations

Anytime I hear a theme, whether it's a rhythm or melody, I like to explore all the different ways I can play a beat with it to shape it. Let's look at punctuating one rhythmic theme, then let's practice some concepts on how to move notes around to be creative in punctuating.

307. **Rhythmic Theme**

Punctuated Beat

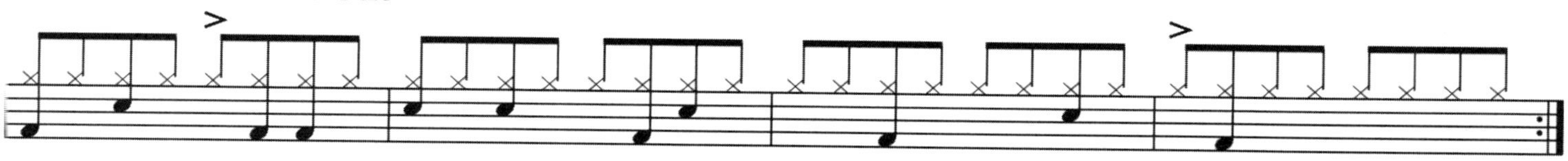

Punctuated concepts with a basic beat:

308.

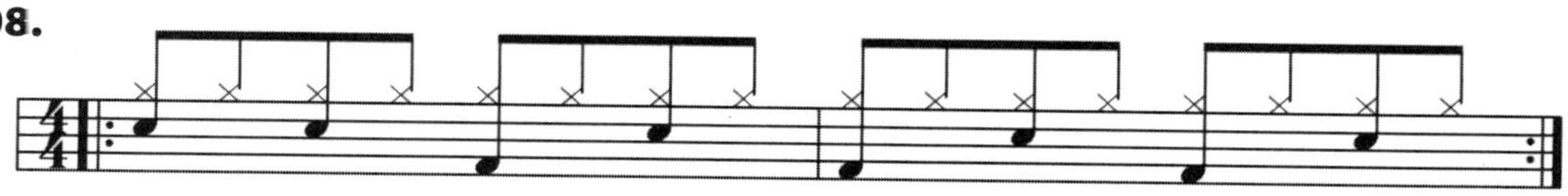

309.

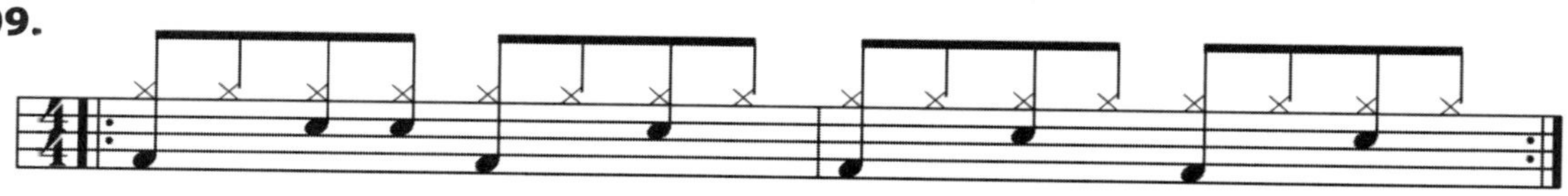

310.

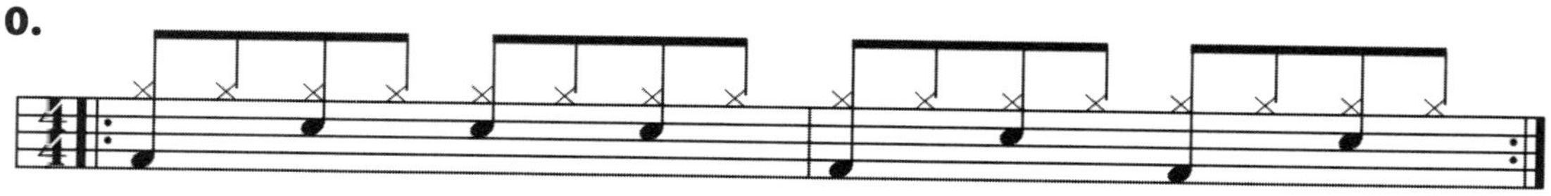

311.

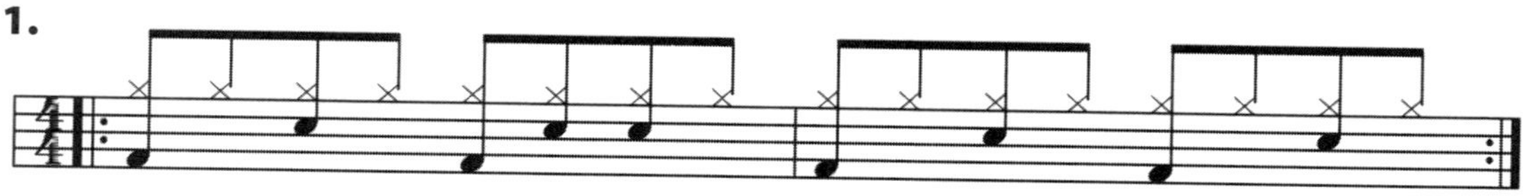

312.

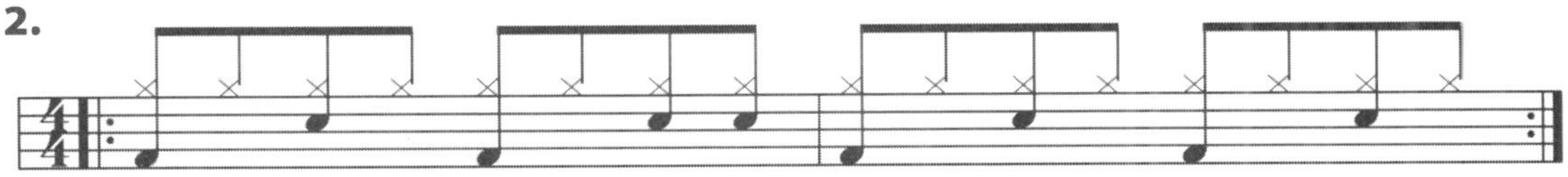

313.

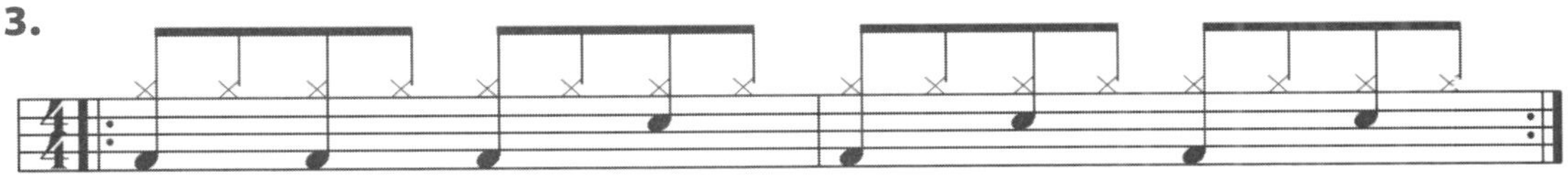

314.

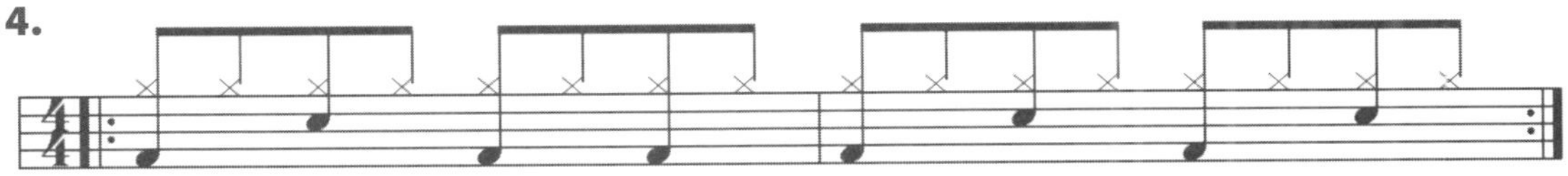

315.

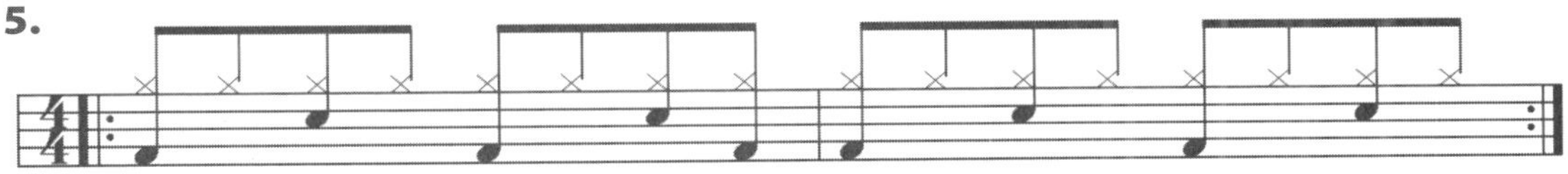

316.

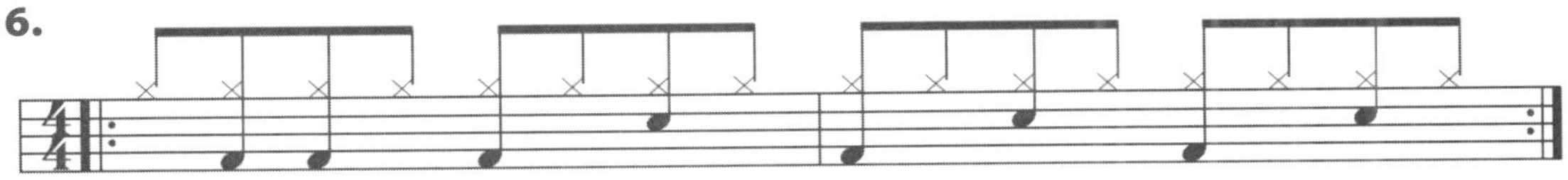

317.

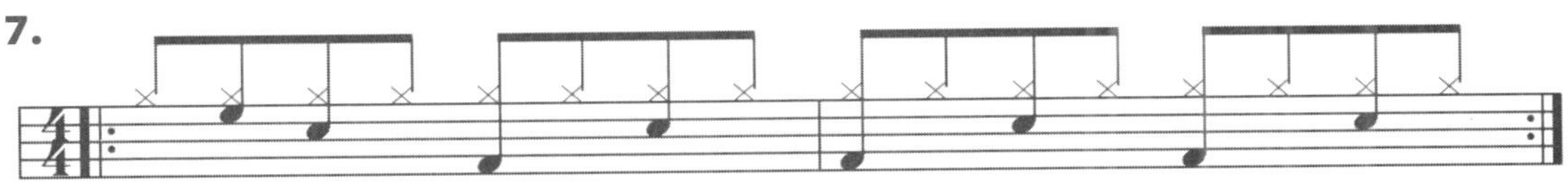

318.

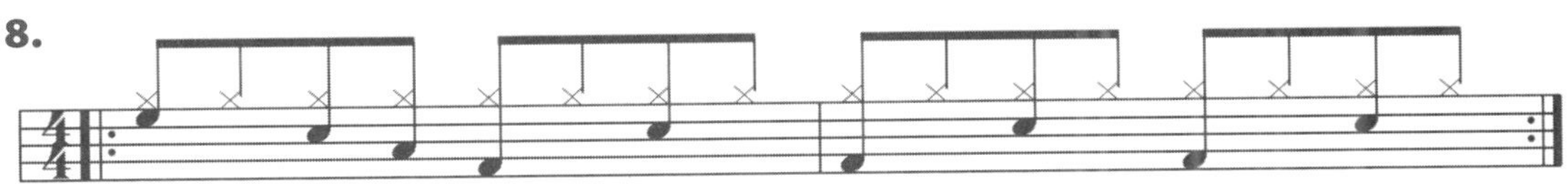

319.

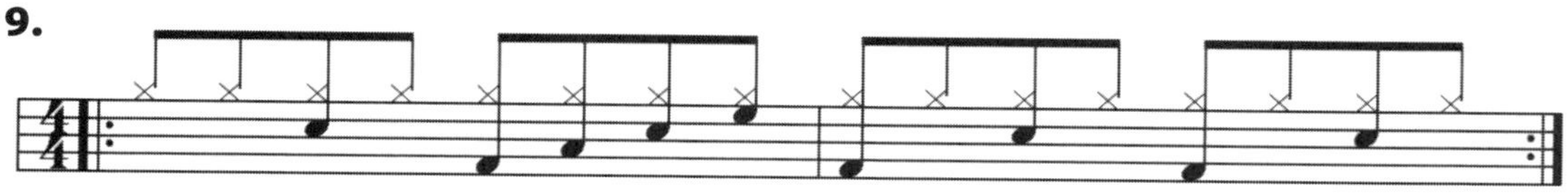

320.

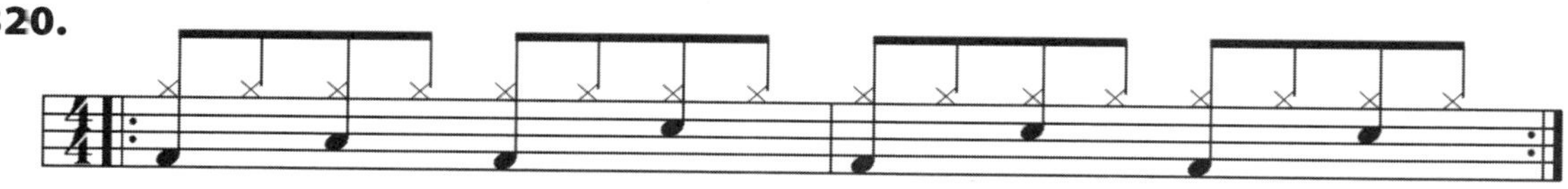

321.

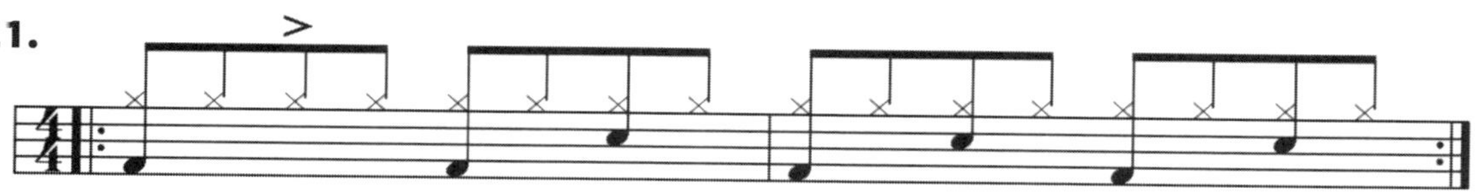

322.

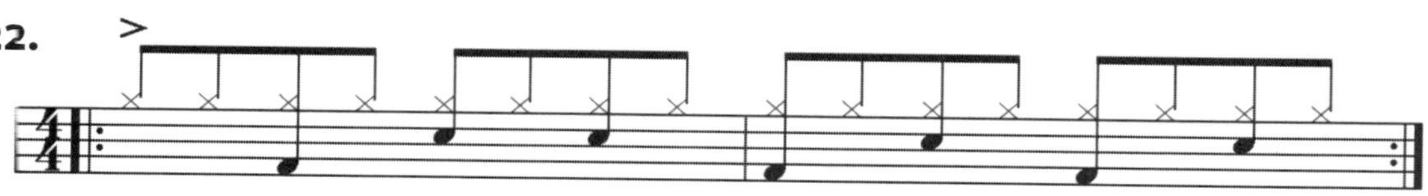

323.

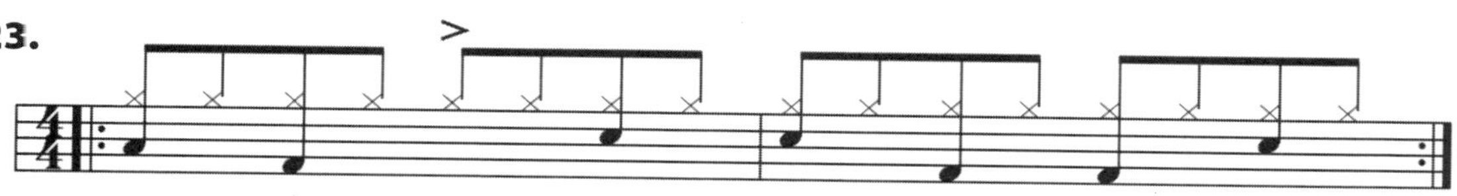

324.

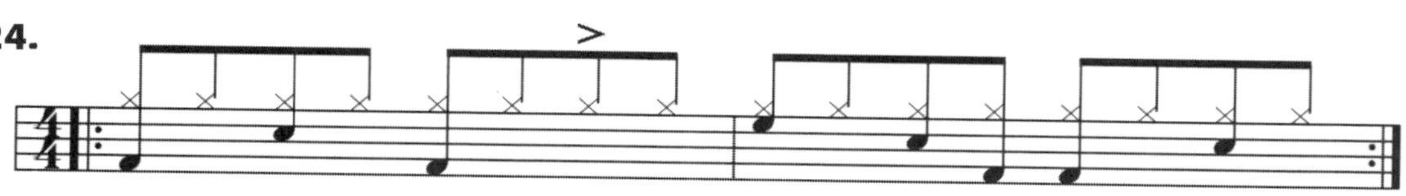

325.

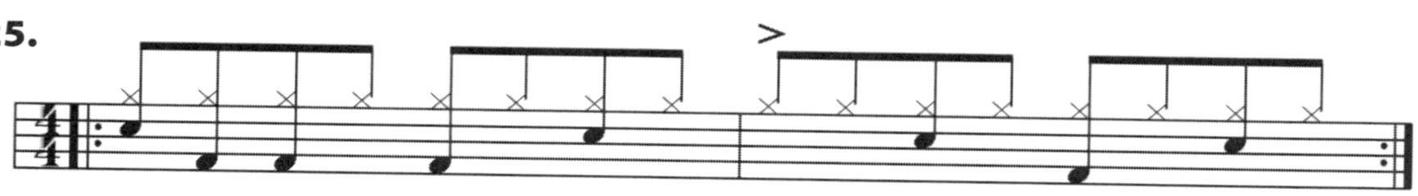

Study #34

Vocabulary

One way to increase your expression is to build up your vocabulary. Some types of music vocabulary are programmed beats, sounds, fills, various songs, singing, different kinds of solos on different instruments, and there are many others. The more vocabulary you have, the more expressive you can be in your playing. Here are some questions to help you see your primary voice, and discover how your vocabulary can expand.

1. What is your favorite genre of music to play?
2. What other styles are incorporated in the music you play the most?
3. What style of music have you not extensively studied?
4. Have you ever gone to a concert to hear a style of music you've never heard before?
5. Have you ever played with a musician who was proficient in a different style than you?
6. What kinds of music do you not like?
7. Which instrument do you like other than drums?
8. Have you ever taken lessons from a person that plays another instrument (other than drums)?
9. Have you ever written music in a genre other than your favorite?
10. How many genres have you studied?
11. Have you ever programmed drums or full beats?
12. Have you ever had to replay a programmed drum part?

These questions are a great way to see where you are in your vocabulary and where it could possibly go. The broader your vocabulary is, the better you can communicate as a musician.

SOLOING

We have arrived at the part everybody loves and that is the drum solo—or is it? Sometimes taking a solo can be the most uncomfortable part of music anyone could ever imagine. I know it used to be that way for me, and sometimes it still can be. When all eyes are on you, what do you do? This section will discuss various principles that can have a drummer always looking forward to this occasion as a happy one when playing any beat.

> "You're never by yourself when taking a solo, your drums are there too."

Often when I play a solo, it is improvised. Even though a solo can be written out and played verbatim or interpreted, I tend to play more solos that are spontaneous and improvised.

Sometimes my approach to soloing is based on my surroundings like my kit, the venue, the musicians I'm playing with, as well as the people in the audience. I like to call this approach "surround playing." From there my goal is to connect with the listener and musically express my ideas to communicate with them. This dialogue can happen in a lot of ways. One way is if the audience is silent, I interpret that as if they are communicating to me that they are listening. I then use that to try and play meaningful ideas that I hope they will connect with. For example, most people understand loud and soft, slow and fast, tempo and no tempo, groove and no groove. I use these basic principles to help me get the music across to them.

If I'm ever at a loss for ideas, what I like to do is rely on everything else to provide the ideas; it doesn't have to all come from me. It could be a bass line, a keyboard run, a guitar chord, someone singing, or even random sounds that may occur. Music is music, no matter where it comes from, and there is an abundance of inspiration everywhere.

Then there are things that I try my best to steer away from when playing an improvised solo. Some of them are overthinking about what I'm going to play, rushing my thoughts, peer or teacher pressure, and being uninspired (to name a few).

The way I deal with those things are to breathe, relax, and become a vehicle for the music to drive while I just enjoy the ride.

Study #35

This is an improvised solo I played on the video.

326.

SOLOING

Study #36

Here is another solo idea that I spontaneously wrote to give you some more ideas on how to build an improvised solo.

327.

AMALGAMATION

Study #37

This section is about you creating and blending all of the things learned throughout this experience. This is just the beginning, but it's a great start. Use the play-along tracks to explore all of the concepts and ideas we've discussed.

Here is a freestyle solo of me putting multiple concepts together.

328.

AMALGAMATION

AMALGAMATION

AMALGAMATION

Study #38

In merging concepts and styles, I discovered that different meters happening at the same time can create some interesting beats. Here we will go through at least four different meters that works well together, creating a cool effect in one beat.

Two Beats in One

329.

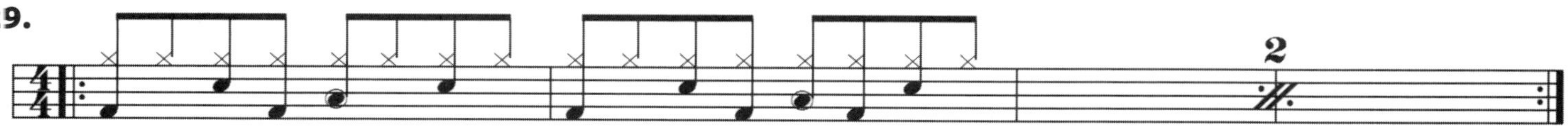

Three Beats in One

330.

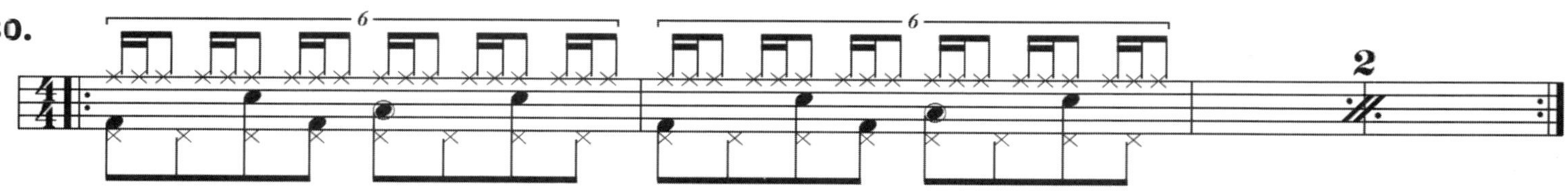

Study #39

These are my "signature beats." Custom beats just for you! I've created these by fusing some of the previous concepts we've studied together. Let's see where you can take some of these ideas and create your own signature beats.

Signature Beat #1

In this groove, I'm playing eighth notes with the right hand and triplets against that with my left foot. The snare and bass drum play a shuffle-type groove against that. This creates an interesting effect, and when coupled with music, it can give the impression of multiple beats happening at the same time.

331.

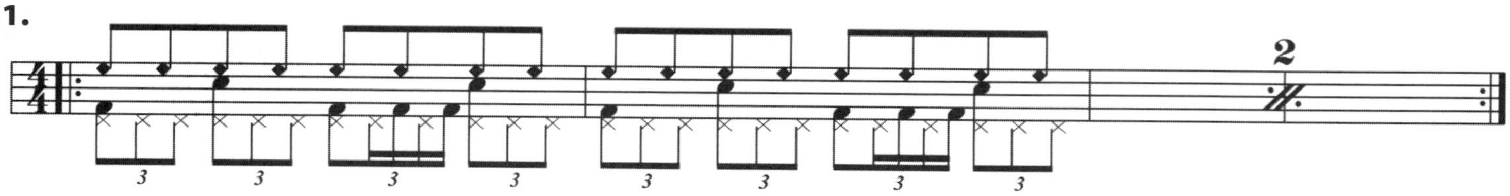

Signature Beat #2

This rhythm is basically a shuffle with the right hand, and then there are two hits on the snare. Then, every beat that the right hand is now playing, the left hand is playing on the hi-hat and on the snare.

332.

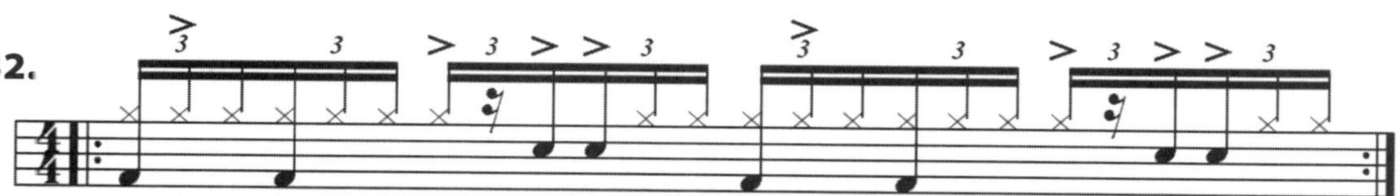

Signature Beat #3

This one was inspired by the great Tony Williams. I spent a lot of time listening to his ride pattern and trying to figure out how he would do it. Tony would go into a double-time kind of figure. I would think, "How is he doing that?" His technique was incredible, but what I saw him do was throw the stick at the cymbal and kind of let the cymbal bounce and then bring it back. So I practiced that technique for quite awhile and eventually thought, "What if I can take some of that concept and apply it to a beat?" Here is what I came up with.

Tony Williams ride cymbal

333.
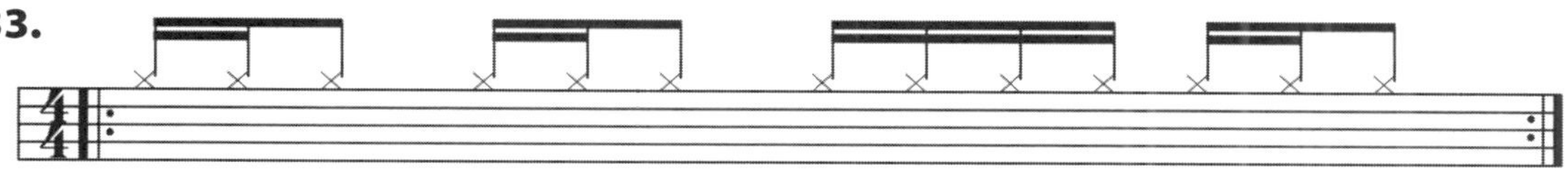

My hi-hat pattern with the beat

334.
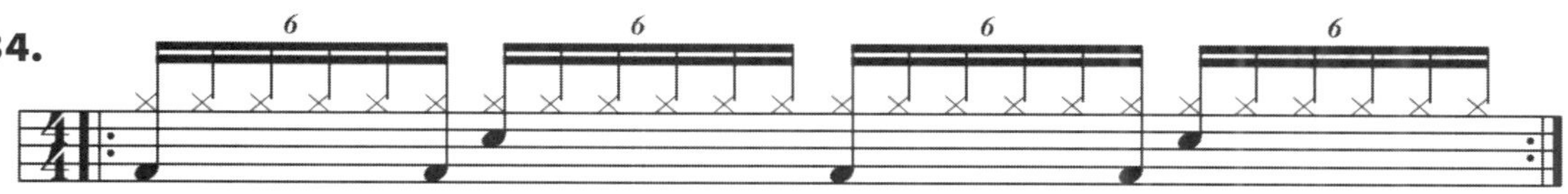

Signature Beat #4

This idea is similar to Signature Beat #3, but I am using machine-like 32nds on the hi-hat with both hands.

335.
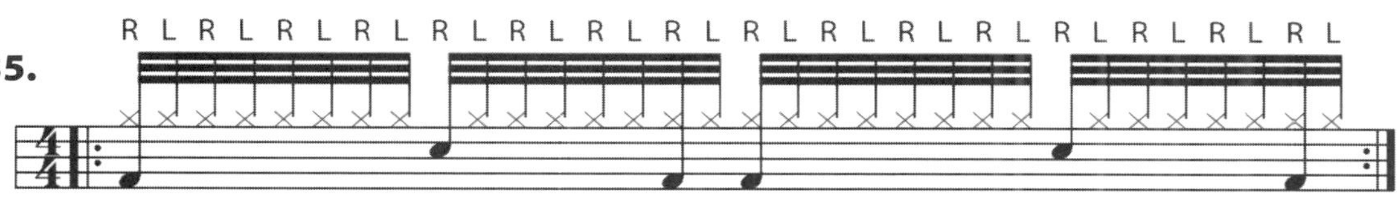

Amalgamation of Signature Beats

On the video I improvised an amalgamation of some of these signature concepts.

336.

AMALGAMATION

PLAY-ALONG

THE CODE

♩ = 89

337.

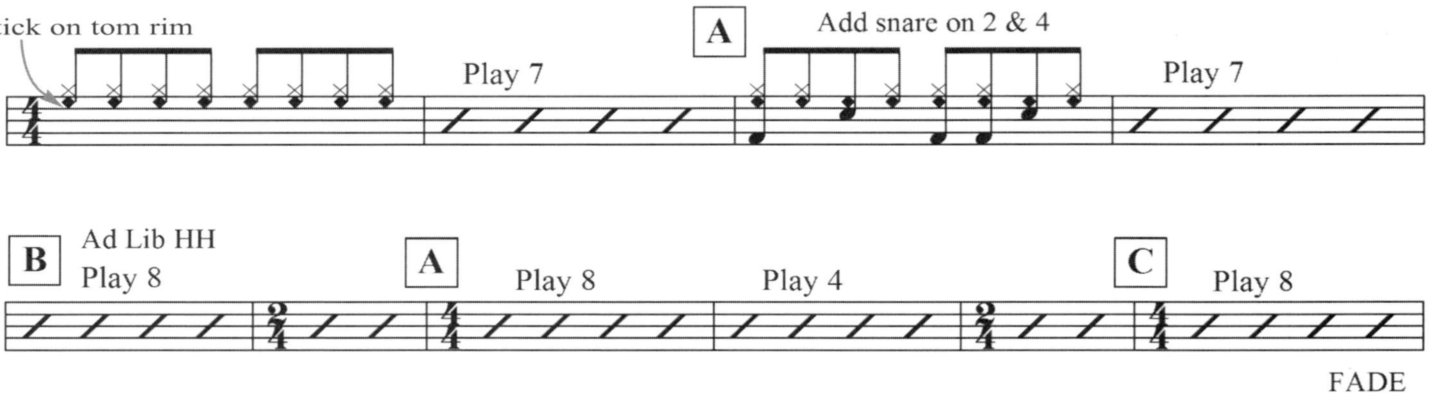

RESOLVED

♪ = 207

338.

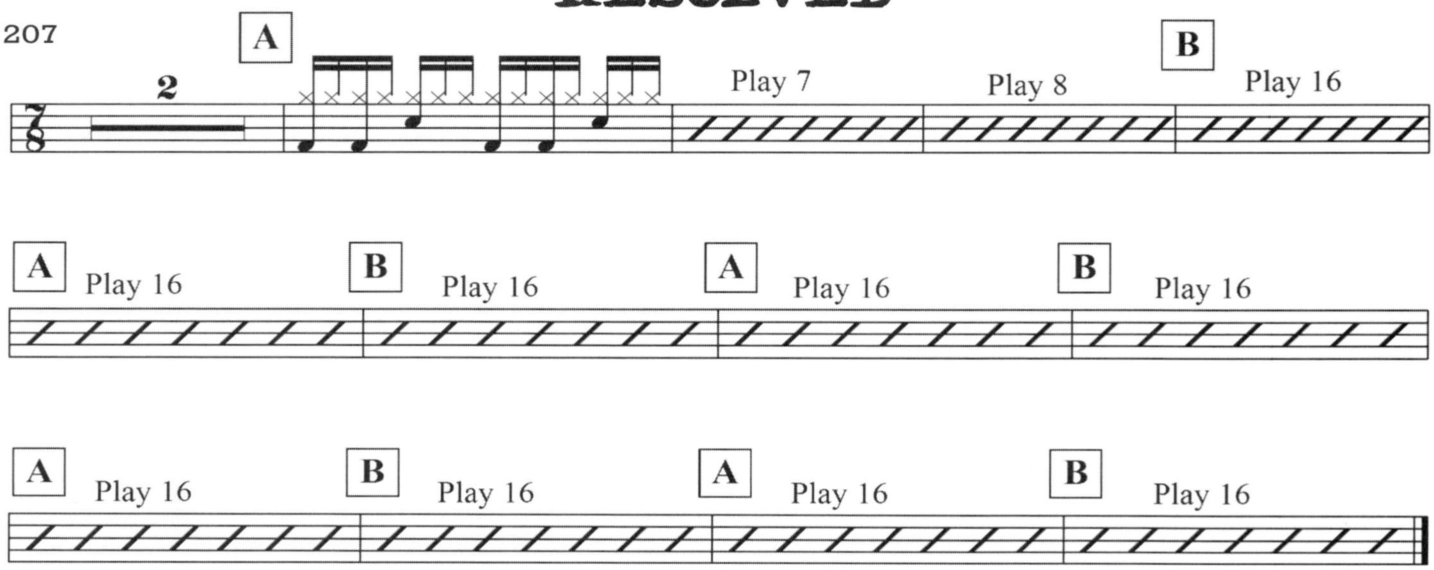

SWAGGESTRY

♩ = 130

339.

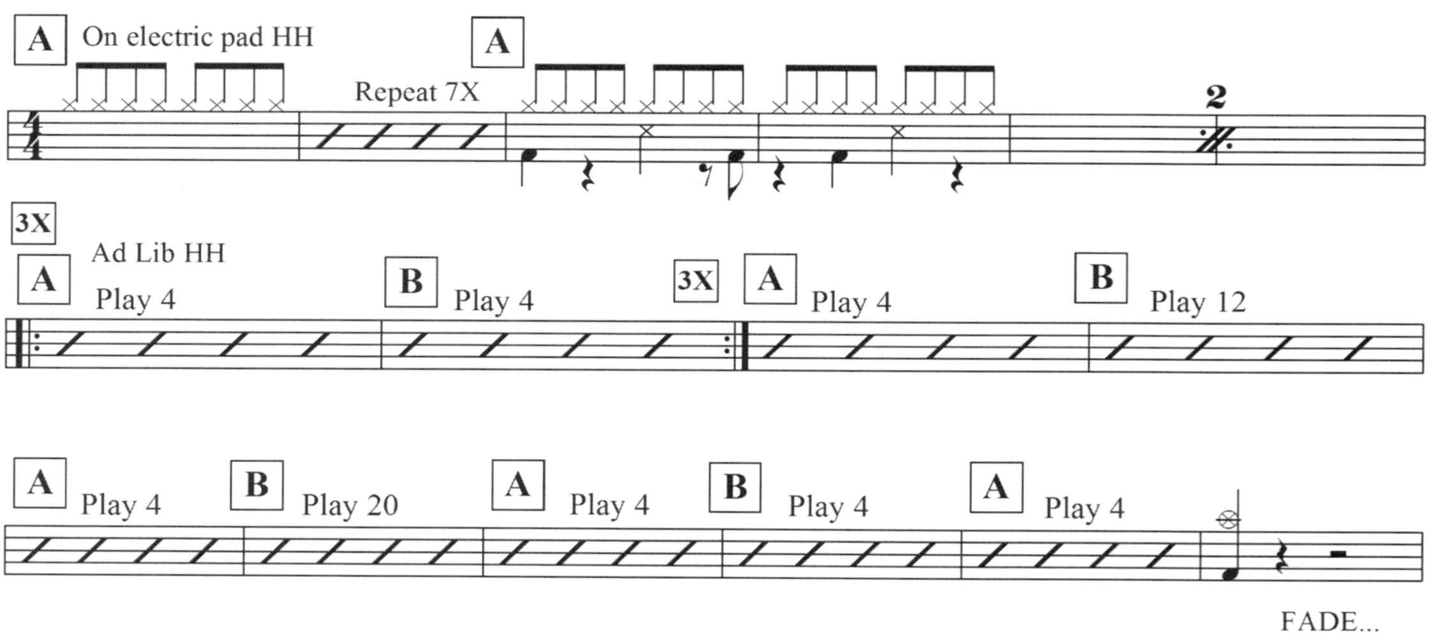

PLAY-ALONG

UNLOCKED

♩ = 97

340.

Intro

Click starts on beat "2"

Light Cymbals

PLAY-ALONG

THE BEAT MATRIX UNLOCKED BPM

Chapter one
Ex. 1- 98 bpm
Ex. 2- 93 bpm
Ex. 3- 107 bpm
Ex. 4- 94 bpm
Ex. 5- 61 bpm
Ex. 6- 91 bpm
Ex. 7- 70 bpm
Ex. 8- 92 bpm
Ex. 9- 114 bpm
Ex. 10- 96 bpm
Warm Up #1
Ex. 11-14- 90 bpm
Warm Up #2
Ex. 15-18- 120 bpm
Ex. 19- 104 bpm
Warm Up #3
Ex. 20-27- 94 bpm
Warm Up #4
Ex. 28-31- 94 bpm
Warm Up #5
Ex. 32- No bpm
Patterns Study#1
Ex. 33- 94 bpm
Ex. 34-35 - 84 bpm
Ex. 36-38 - 92 bpm
Patterns Study #2
Ex. 39-42 - 102 bpm
Patterns Study #3
Ex. 43-48 - 90 bpm
Patterns Study #4
Ex. 49-54 - 90 bpm
Patterns Study #5
Ex. 55-57 - No bpm
Ex. 58- 117 bpm
Ex. 59-61 - 97 bpm
Patterns Study #6
Ex. 62-63- 92 bpm
Ex. 64- 87 bpm
Patterns Study #7
Ex. 65-67 - 97 bpm
Patterns Study #8
Ex. 68-70 - 92 bpm
Sonics Study #9
Ex. 71-74 - 92 bpm
Sonics Study #10
Ex. 75-78
slow - 80 bpm
medium- 115 bpm
Fast- 189 bpm
(All three bpm's for each exercise)
Sonics Study #11
Ex. 79-88 - 92 bpm
Sonics Study #12
Ex. 89-95 - 94 bpm
Sonics Study #13
Ex. 96-101 - 94 bpm
Musical Swag Study #14
Ex. 102-106 -94 bpm
Musical Swag Study #15
Ex. 107-109 - 92 bpm
Ex. 110- 157 bpm
Ex. 111-117 - 94 bpm
Musical Swag Study #16
Ex. 118 - 97 bpm
Ex. 119- 120 - 92 bpm
Ex. 121 - 87 bpm
Musical Swag Study #17
Ex. 122-126 - 92 bpm
Performance Study #18
Ex. 127-147 - 94 bpm
Ex. 148-157 - 90 bpm
Ex. 158-162 - 89 bpm
Ex. 163- 167- 92 bpm
Performance Study #19
Ex. 168 - 92 bpm
Performance Study #20
Ex. 169-174 - 94 bpm
Performance Study #21
Ex. A-G - 87 bpm
Improvisation Study #22
Ex. 175-184 - 102 bpm
Ex. 185-189 - 85 bpm
Improv. Study #23
Ex. 190-194- 90 bpm
Improv. Study #24
Ex. 195-200 - 90 bpm
Improv. Study #25
Ex. 201-205 - No bpm
Improv. Study #26
Ex. 206- 209 - 95 bpm
Ex. 210 - 211 - 92 bpm
Improv. Study #27
Ex. 212-215 - 90 bpm
Chop Class Study #28
Ex. 216-234- 87 bpm
Chop Class Study #29
Ex. 235-253- 80 bpm
Chop Class Study #30
Ex. 254-259 - 87 bpm
Chop Class Study #31
Ex. 260-297 - 90 bpm
Chop Class Study #32
Ex. 298- 306 - 95 bpm
Chop Class Study #33
Ex. 307-325 - 87 bpm
Soloing Study #35
Ex. 326-329 - 90 bpm
Study #36-37
N/A
Soloing Study #38
Ex. 331-333 - 93 bpm
Soloing/Amalgamation Study #39-41
N/A
Amalgamation Study #42 (Signature Beats)
From the video (There are 5) - about 90 bpm
777-93-11 from the video about 115 bpm
The 10 Beat Essentials Study#43/44
Ex. 1-6- 100 bpm
Ex. 7-8 - 157 bpm
Ex. 9 - 130 bpm
Ex. 10 - 180 bpm

THANK YOU'S

First, thank you God for the opportunity to share what has been given to me.

To you the reader:

The words and performances in this book wouldn't mean much if it wasn't for you. Thank you for your support, positivity, and love for drums. Much love to you.

To my Mother who is resting, I would have never been able to do anything if it wasn't for all of your sacrifices, encouraging words when I wanted to quit, lifestyle, teachings, and just your unwavering, unfailing love. I've never encountered anyone like you in all of my life, a true angel. I'll love and represent always.

To my family, the sky is limit for you guys and you keep me pushing, I love y'all endlessly! My Sis. niece, and nephew, thank you for all of your great support. To the "Deacon" this is a result of you investing in me, I'm forever grateful for you.

To Rob, Joe, Al, Rick, Willie, and everyone at Hudson. Thank you very much for having the patience, vision and faith to see this through! And to all the participants on this project, your work is priceless and greatly valued.

To GC's for holding me down, forever smiles with the biggest heart!

Blair Wells and Chris Sholar, true geniuses and friends, couldn't have done this without you. THANK YOU!

To all of the companies and friends for their absolute genuine support: Yamaha Family Greg, Daryl, Pru, and everyone. Zildjian Family Debbie and Craigie, Sarah, Emily, Paul, Jeff, Aaron, Chris, Anna, John D. and everyone. Remo Family, Chris Hart and everyone, Vater Family Chad Brandonlini and everyone, Armed & Dangerous Family, and Joe Testa, I really appreciate your zeal and support man.

Last but not least to all of the artists, musicians (especially drummers) and friends who have ever crossed my path, inspired, supported me, and anyone who has ever believed in me in spite of all the odds, a magnanimous thank you to you!

MORE BEAT MATRIX CONTENT

AVAILABLE FOR SEPARATE PURCHASE

Play-Alongs, Drum Loops, and Sample Libraries

Additional Material available at hudsonmusic.com

It's always very important to have the proper tools to excel in studying for growth and to prepare for the big musical moments. So, in addition to the book and video, I've produced and performed (with special guest artist, producer, and guitarist Chris Sholar) a 12-song play-along set, displaying at least 7 different musical vibes, with and without drums (four of these are included with this book; the others are available separately). This is to help aid you in practicing and creating the beat music concepts presented in this project, as well as for listening purposes.

To expand the base even more, I've also added 30 mixed and mastered drum loops, covering 5 distinct styles (trap, drum'n'bass, hip-hop, '70s disco/ rock, and gospel) with 5 different kit configurations. You can also use this to assist with practicing, as well as writing, sampling, producing and creating music on and off the kit. This also works well used with other instruments.

Have fun exploring, mixing, matching, soloing, producing and playing with these as far as your imagination can take you, unlocking your full potential. I look forward to seeing and hearing what you do with it!

Play-Along Guide

- Code - The secret is in the feel.
- Resolved - Imagination is the key.
- Swaggestry - The bounce effect.
- Unlocked - Open up.
- Light Speed - Rhythm is a Dance.
- Beat Tables - Knock knock is the answer.
- Afro Math - Feel the one.
- Circle Squared - Explore the equations.
- BPM - Speed versus slow.
- Juxtapose - Inside and outside the grid.
- Vibes - Driving.
- Technodrum - Technology meets drums.

The Drum Loop/Sample Specs

- File Format: .wav
- Instant Download
- Samples (5 Full Kits)
- Loops (30 loops, 5 styles)
- Sound Quality 24 Bit 44.1kHz

AVAILABLE SEPARATELY: Play-Alongs/Loops/Sample Kits

Play-Along Tracks (audio only)

5. Light Speed
6. Beat Tables
7. Afro Math
8. Circle Squared
9. BPM
10. Juxtapose
11. Vibes
12. Technodrum

Loops

30 Loops w/BPMs
5 Different Categories:

- Trap
- Hip Hop
- Gospel
- Drum 'n' Bass
- '70s/Disco/Rock

Sample Kits

5 different genre full sample kits